Musical Story Hours

Musical Story Hours

Using Music with Storytelling and Puppetry

William M. Painter

With a foreword by
Spencer Shaw

Library Professional Publications
1989

Printed in the United States of America

The paper used in this publication meets the minimum
requirements of American National Standard for Information
Sciences—Permanence of Paper for Printed Library Materials,
ANSI Z39.48-1984. ∞

Library of Congress Cataloging in Publication Data

Painter, William M., 1941–
Musical story hours : using music with storytelling and
puppetry / William M. Painter ; with a foreword by Spencer Shaw.
p. cm.
Includes bibliographies. ISBN 0–208-02205–8.
1. Storytelling. 2. Libraries, Children's—Activity programs.
3. Puppets and puppet–plays in education. 4. Music in education.
5. Children—Books and reading. I. Title.
Z718.3.P34   1989   027.62′51—dc 19   88-31446
                                                    CIP

Contents

Acknowledgments

I would like to thank the people who have offered their help, advice, and encouragement for this book: Gloria Zavish, Patricia Landers, Ilene Zaleski, Gerry Richman and Ceil Mooney of the North Miami Public Library; Anne Boegen, Coordinator of Children's Services, Miami Dade Public Library; Virginia Mathews of The Shoe String Press; my daughters, Jeannie and Jill; and my parents, William and Margaret. For the photograph: James L. Linn; for typing the manuscript: my wife, Melanie; and for fixing the typewriter—several times!—my son, Carl.

Foreword

Fundamental to the success of a library's services to its patrons are the *quantity* and *quality* of offered programs that meet diverse interests, needs, and concerns. Since its inception, library service for youth has been enriched with traditional programs of storytelling. Through this art form, librarians have shared the oral lore gathered from the many cultures of the world. They have provided imaginary journeys into realms of modern fairy tales and fantasy and have extracted the contents of realistic stories in their tellings. With an artistic blend of texts and illustrations, storytellers have incorporated picture books in programs for the youngest listeners. For all ages, they have enhanced their presentations with poetry.

Blended from many cultures and through many centuries, storytelling has developed into a disciplined art. Over the years, those who narrated infused their tellings with the voice, and, depending upon their cultural heritage, accompanied the verbal renditions with dance, chants, or an instrument. The insertion of these components heightened the effect when audiences responded emotionally to the rhythmic flow of music. Storytellers and listeners became mutually involved, for they experienced sensory pleasure in listening and in stimulated body movements. From such early beginnings a bridge was forged to link the past with the present.

Today, some of these same approaches are still an indigenous ingredient of storytelling in various cultures. For the librarian who wishes to combine the telling with music, alternative approaches are utilized. Some may use an instrument such as an autoharp, a recorder, a flute, a dulcimer, or a guitar. With advances in technology, the creative integration of carefully selected recordings and/or cassette tapes provides possibilities for extended dimensions in presenting storytelling programs. It is the latter method that the author expounds in his *Musical Story Hours: Using Music with Storytelling and Puppetry.* With simplicity and clarity he establishes his rationale for the use of musical recordings as an innovative and effective way to bring books and stories into children's lives:

> It helps create a mood. It stimulates and holds interest, and, somehow, quiets and focuses audiences' attention. It can enable librarians, teachers, or puppeteers to work with younger audiences by extending their attention spans. It helps cultivate a lifelong skill and interest in reading, in stories, in books, and in using libraries. And it certainly adds an element of cultural enrichment by exposing very young children to good music. . . . the use of music is enriching and fun.

Such noteworthy principles are achieveable if, *first,* a librarian masters the essential techniques of storytelling and maintains this artistic skill in library programming; *second,* the teller reads and becomes conversant with a broad background of literature (oral and literary forms) from which selections may be made for appropriate age and/or interest groups; *third,* the librarian knows the fundamentals of program planning, particularly as it relates to the art of storytelling. This knowledge of program planning embodies an understanding of some of the purposes and values of such activities in relationship to contemporary audiences and the primary components of a storytelling session. Finally, the integration of recordings requires a knowledge of specific types of music that may be compatible with selected stories in terms of *theme, mood, and tempo.*

One of the primary objectives of a library storytelling program is to introduce listeners to the inexhaustible store of literature. Therefore, in the preparation of the activity, the selection of stories must initiate the process and have the highest priority. This procedure requires answers to pertinent questions. Will the material satisfy the interests and age levels of the intended audience? Do the selected stories need the implementation of musical accompaniment to extract the desired response? Indeed, is it always necessary or advisable to have the supplementary integration of music for some of the shared narratives? When a story possesses vivid imagery in terms of theme, plot, setting, characterization, language, and style, other extraneous elements may intrude. Will appeals to several stimuli (auditory, visual, kinesthetic) divert the focus of the listeners' attention from the verbal presentation? Within such a context a careful balance must be sustained with the use of musical recordings for some stories and none for others.

The author's extensive knowledge of classical music has enabled him to suggest appropriate musical selections for specific types of programs and for individual stories. Drawing upon his personal experiences, he provides creative, sensitively developed techniques, suggested thematic programs, bibliographies, and discographies. Such guidelines will enable a storyteller to embark upon another adventure in library programming with the use of recorded music. Recognizing storytelling as a creative art form, tellers may respond to a story and interpret it differently one from another. In a similar manner the subjective responses to a particular recording may cause a storyteller to consider a selection different from the suggested composition. This does not lessen the effectiveness of the author's approach. Rather, it indicates creative forces at work within a teller who is establishing an empathic relationship with the story and the harmonious melody of a musical composition.

The author refers to an article that I published thirty years ago entitled "Recorded Magic for Story Hours," in *Top of the News*. The questions that were propounded then are still pertinent today. In the use of recordings: (a) Will it help to motivate and provide a bridge to literature? (b) Will it give pleasure and entertain? (c) Will it educate by providing a means for personal, social, and intellectual growth? (d) Will it appeal esthetically by enabling listeners to intensify their search for beauty? I would also add to these queries one more. (e) Will it help audiences to perceive the interconnections of cultural inheritances through the sharing of music from different spheres? It is acknowledged

that these concerns are considered by the author who explores
them diligently and with perceptive insights.

Spencer G. Shaw
Professor Emeritus
Graduate School of Library
and Information Science
University of Washington
Seattle, Washington

1.

Introduction: Why Add Music?

The whys and hows of using mood-creating music with storytelling and puppetry

I have a great idea for all of us who work with children in libraries, elementary schools, and nursery schools. Parents and grandparents, aunts and uncles can use it at home just as well. In fact, anyone interested in bringing books and stories to life creatively for children can experiment with thousands of variations of this basic idea: putting stories and music together.

Some years ago, I started using some rather unusual cassette tapes as background music for some stories being told to two- and three-year-olds. If you look over the following music list, your first reaction may be negative and disbelieving:

Handel,	Concerto for Harp and Orchestra in B-flat Major; First Movement (5:35)
Bach,	Suite for Harp, First Movement. (3:53)
Mozart,	Adagio and Rondo in C Minor (11:00)
Wagenseil,	Concerto for Harp and Orchestra, Second Movement (5:00)

"You've got to be kidding," you say? Not at all. The truth is that, once you're over the initial shock, there is absolutely nothing more practical and magical than music to back up and enhance your storytelling to children. Just within the range of the four classical pieces listed, there are such variations of mood and emotion (and playing times) that the story-matching possibilities are endless.

Picture a group of about twenty-five two-and three-year-olds sitting on mats in front of a large puppet stage with a three-

1

by-nine-foot window. Their mothers are sitting in back of the children, in chairs. The puppet stage lights up and the auditorium goes dark. The librarian sits on a high wooden stool with a book, held in the light, in front of the puppet stage. The volunteers are ready inside the stage—Sam, a retired widower, Jack, another retiree, Fereydoun, a father of four who used to appear on children's television shows in Iran before leaving there ten years ago. At the right moment, Fereydoun slips the Handel Harp Concerto into the tape player. The piece takes five minutes and thirty-five seconds, so the telling of *Harry the Dirty Dog* has been rehearsed and embellished to finish in a tie with Handel. The puppeteers do not have very elaborate movements to perform, but they follow along as Harry hops from his house to the road to the railroad station—getting dirtier all the while. The gentle, bouncy harp music does not obtrude at all. The music helps set the emotional tone of the story, and twenty-five toddlers and parents are spellbound. The music is a large part of their rapt attention. The initial discovery that this music could help to keep the attention of two- and three-year-olds (and sometimes one-year-olds) over the course of a half an hour, twice a week, throughout four months of programs amazed me, too.

The music and puppets enable us to work with younger children than many libraries like to start with. As the "babies" get older and reach school age, parents often tell us, the early experience with books, stories, and the library gives these children a head start when it is time to learn letters, numbers, and words. There are a number of scholarly articles in education and library literature about the reading-readiness effect of such programming; the real impact, however, comes when you hear it from the parents.

Most of these parents had taken home armloads of picture books after each story hour, which is a prime reason libraries should offer these programs. The combination of librarians and parents both bringing books into the lives of very young children is pretty hard to beat.

One point to be stressed here is that the idea of using music with stories is not limited to librarians or others who have puppet stages. Parents with a phonograph or cassette player and a bed or couch can do many of these things as well; elementary and nursery school teachers can use these ideas and each chapter's sample program as a way to add creative variety and interest to their teaching. Most college education textbooks stress the importance of variety at all levels of classroom teaching.

This book emphasizes the use of classical music, simply because the emotional nuances offered by classical music provide more options than do other types. However, there are also discussions of other forms of music as well—dixieland, swing, marches, ballet, solo instrumental, western, folk melodies, polkas, and novelty music. Discussions of traditional children's music is, in general, not included. Much has been written on that, but no one seems to have tried exploring what Jean-Pierre Rampal's flute could do for story hours, or what Ruth Welcome's zither could add.

The fun thing about all of this is that people working with children can take the ideas presented here and experiment with their own match-ups. They may find that the pairings used in the book are perfectly suited to them, or they may prefer the thrill of the hunt, these ideas inspiring them to dig into their old record and tape collections, library music holdings, and record stores for others.

The main thing is that those who are interested in bringing books and stories into children's lives are always looking for innovative and effective ways to do so. The ideas in this book work. The results and influences, which may be years down the road, indicate the seriousness and importance of such efforts.

The puppet involvement mentioned in the sample programs for each chapter is very simple, with hardly any props needed. The puppets are completely optional, depending on what you wish to do or what is available. I keep the puppetry simple because I do two, three, or four programs a week, and we don't have time or staff to create elaborate props. If your situation is different, you may wish to use more props.

As stated earlier, music helps to create and hold interest, greatly enhancing and facilitating effective work with younger children. Other reasons for liberally adding music will also be explored in this book. One is that music helps create the mood of a story. Another is that music helps to describe the personality of a character in the story. The harp music mentioned earlier, for example, is playful, cheerful, mischievous, and instantly understood by a two-year-old as well as by a thirty-year-old. Music can add a needed element of surprise to a story rendition. Finally, the use of music is enriching and fun. Consider: this may be one of the few times some of the children are exposed to music other than that of Twisted Sister and The Rolling Stones! These are all positive and compelling reasons for trying this multi-media approach.

I was amused recently in reading a biography of the composer Haydn, to come across a description of such a program at one of Austrian Express Maria Theresa's social gatherings in the mid-1700s. "Papa" Haydn delighted an audience of several hundred with a performance of his opera, *Philemon and Baucis*, using a marionette theater, musicians and opera singers behind the stage, and a story based on Greek mythology. A real musical story hour!

For quick reference, at the end of this book, you will find a chapter-by-chapter listing of the pairings of music and stories discussed throughout the text. The list should simplify the ideas for you, and make them easy to use. Remember, though, that you can also take these pairings as examples or guides, and find similar, effective pairings on your own. That is indeed part of the fun.

Schwann's Record and Tape Guide, which is updated quarterly, can be of great help to you in searching out your own musical choices. (ABC Consumer Magazine, Capitol Cities, ABC Inc., 825 7th Avenue, New York, New York 10019).

Books like the American Library Association's *Storytellling with Puppets* (ALA, 1985) will give you ideas for making your own puppets and using them creatively. If time is limited, you may prefer to purchase puppets from toy stores, department stores, gift shops, or directly from the manufacturers. Dakin, Inc. (P.O. Box 7200, San Francisco, California 94120–9977) and Country Critters, Inc. (217 Neosho Street, Burlington, Kansas 66839) are two top-notch makers of hand puppets. There are others, such as Russ Berrie and Co., Inc. (111 Bauer Drive,

Oakland, New Jersey 07436) and Applause (6101 Variel Avenue, Woodland Mills, California 91367), which are also very good.

Books like *Monkey Mitt Rhymes* by the Wizard of Ahhs (P.O. Box 851, Pollock Pines, California 95726) and *Mitt Magic* by Lynda Roberts (Gryphon Press, 1985) will supply you with plenty of finger plays and activity games.

You may wish to tape record entire programs' background music, in order, rather than "fish" for the correct spot on a record. This would help you store programs for future use as well.

As the book will point out, there are many ways to bring about combinations of music, storytelling, puppetry and activities.

Sample Musical Story Hour
Theme: Dogs

1. Participation Song: "Bingo"

   There was a farmer who had a dog
   and Bingo was his name-O
   B-I-N-G-O
   B-I-N-G-O
   B-I-N-G-O
   And Bingo was his name-O

   (As you sing other verses, take away one letter for each verse and substitute a clap for each letter, to the rhythm of the song. At the end, five rhythmic claps replace the five letters.)

   Puppet Participation:

   If you have a dog puppet to represent Bingo, he can be made to dance along to the singing.

2. Participation Song: "If You're Happy and You Know It"

   If you're happy and you know it, clap your hands
   If you're happy and you know it, clap your hands

If you're happy and you know it, then your face will surely
    show it
If you're happy and you know it, clap your hands

If you're happy and you know it, stamp your feet
If you're happy and you know it, stamp your feet
If you're happy and you know it, then you face will surely
    show it
If you're happy and you know it, stamp your feet

If you're happy and you know it, shout "Hooray!"
If you're happy and you know it, shout "Hooray!"
If you're happy and you know it, then your face will surely
    show it
If you're happy and you know it, shout "Hooray!"

If you're happy and you know it, do all three
    (Clap, stamp, shout "Hooray!")
If you're happy and you know it, do all three
If you're happy and you know it, then your face will surely
    show it
If you're happy and you know it, do all three.

Puppet Participation:

If you have a dog puppet with feet, you or an assistant
(possibly behind a puppet stage, if you have one) can make
it clap, stamp, and shout along with you and the children.
    Tell the children: "Speaking of being happy, we're going
to have a story about a happy little dog now. He's called
Harry the dirty dog, and he's happy most of the time—
except when he has to TAKE A BATH!" This leads right into
the story. If you have a white dog puppet, you can add
some black spots with charcoal; if you have a black dog, add
white spots (chalk) and the puppeteer can bring up both
"Harrys" as you tell the story.

3. Musical Story:

Story: *Harry the Dirty Dog* by Gene Zion
Music: Handel's Concerto for Harp and Orchestra in a
           B-flat Major, first movement.

Musical   Whatever music you choose should be light,
Mood: bouncy, upbeat, and melodious. Harp music in
            general seems to work well, unless it's an adagio
            (slow) movement. The first movement of the
            Handel Harp Concerto is perfect, but you can
            search out other harp pieces, or other instru-
            ments, that set the tone equally as well.

4. Filmstrip:

Weston Woods Co. produces an extensive collection of excellent filmstrips based on children's stories. These provide a
nice change of pace and add variety to your program. Since
we're using a general theme of dogs here, you could bring
in the filmstrip, *Finders Keepers,* which is based on the
humorous Caldecott-Award-winning book about two dogs
fighting over which one owns the bone they both discovered.

Special Considerations:

If you can, use a microphone for yourself. This puts your
storytelling well above the background music. If you don't
have a microphone, keep the record player or cassette player
behind a puppet stage, off to the side, or somewhere in the
background. Your voice should be the dominant sound; the
music backs you up.

5. Activity:

Coloring is an activity which the youngest of children can
enjoy. If you manage to come up with about fifteen separate
boxes of crayons, plenty of newspaper to put down on the
floor, and something to color which is related to your program, you can make thirty pre-schoolers happy for about
ten minutes.

If you can draw a dog (anything close!) to represent
Bingo, or your happy-and-you-know-it puppet, or a charac-

ter from your story, you could photocopy thirty copies to distribute.

The children can take home a memento of the program. My suggestion that "You can tape the drawing to your refrigerator!" has become a standing joke in North Miami. Dozens of parents come back and laugh, after about ten weeks, "You should SEE my refrigerator! I'm going to have to buy another one to hold more pictures!"

Other Dog Stories for Parents and Children to Share at Home (or for Storytelling)

Biro, Val. *Gumdrop and the Great Sausage Caper.* Gareth Stevens, 1985.

Carlson, Natalie. *Harriet and the Garden.* Carolrhoda, 1982.

Charles, Donald. *Shaggy Dog's Tall Tale.* Children's Press, 1980.

Cleary, Beverly. *Two Dog Biscuits.* Morrow, 1966.

De Fossard, Esta. *Dinah, the Dog with a Difference.* Gareth Stevens, 1985.

Dodd, Lynley. *Hairy Maclary from Donaldson's Dairy.* Gareth Stevens, 1983.

Gackenbach, Dick. *Dog for a Day.* Clarion, 1987.

Graham, Margaret Bloy. *Benjy's Dog House.* Harper and Row, 1973.

Jordan, June. *Kimako's Story.* Houghton Mifflin, 1981.

Morris, Terry. *Lucky Puppy, Lucky Boy.* Knopf, 1980.

Thayer, Jane. *The Puppy Who Wanted a Boy.* Morrow, 1985.

Zion, Gene. *Harry and the Lady Next Door.* Harper and Row, 1960.

References

Cassette Tape:

Handel, George Frederick. Concerto for Harp and Orchestra in B-flat Major. First movement. *The Harmonious Harp: Concert*

Favorites by Bach, Handel, Mozart and Others. Deutsche Grammophon 413684-4; and *Harp Concertos.* London/Treasury 414 052-4.

Book:

Zion, Gene. *Harry the Dirty Dog.* Harper and Row, 1956.

The author in action with volunteer puppeteers (l. to r.) Annahitta Moghimi-Kian, Tammy and Laurel Sessions, daughter Jill Painter and Sasha Moghimi-Kian.

2.

A Case History

How we added classical flute music to
a story-and-puppet version of *Monkey Face*

Your use of musical background does not have to be as
involved as in the following particular case. However, if you
have plenty of time and want to see how good you can really
become at this, you can do something similar to our orchestration of Frank Asch's story, *Monkey Face*.

First of all, let's examine the characters and events of the
story. The little monkey draws a picture of his mother and
wants to show it to his friends before unveiling it to her. He
takes it to the rabbit, the owl, the crocodile, the elephant, the
giraffe, and the lion. Each animal offers his own bit of aesthetic
criticism to the artistic young monkey. The rabbit says it's a fine
portrait, but it needs longer ears. The owl stares wisely at the
creation before suggesting that bigger eyes would make it look
more like the mother. The crocodile grins with real admiration,
but he's sure it needs more teeth. The elephant looks carefully
over the drawing, with all the newly added improvements, and
says that a longer nose would surely result in a still better
likeness. The lion points out this mature monkey mother obviously should have more hair on her head. The giraffe naturally
points out that the neck needs some lengthening.

If you have not seen the book, you can imagine what the
finished portrait looked like. If you know mothers, you can also
imagine that her reaction to the picture was to praise it to the
skies, hang it up for all to see and assure her boy that no further
changes are necessary. In short, she loves it just the way it is.

I obviously wanted some warm and gentle music to back

my telling of this story. Yet each distinct anecdote within the story had its own special flavor.

I found several collections of flute music played by Jean-Pierre Rampal, many of which were perfectly suitable to serve as general background music for this story. However, I found one in particular which seemed to divide itself up into the exact number of segments to go with the anecdotes within the story. Miraculously, each segment seemed to fit the tone I wanted to set—including a slow, lumbering section for the elephant. The piece was "Variations on a Theme by Rossini," by Chopin. The match-up seemed to be made in heaven, but of course it took several hours of listening before I found such a perfect combination.

It is really not necessary to get that specific about every segment of a story. Perhaps for a special occasion or if the creative mood sweeps you away and time allows, you could try something very satisfying like this. One must be realistic. Most librarians are working with understaffing as a way of life. Time to be creative is extremely limited. Periods of concentration are few and precious, but sometimes being able to get something as perfect as possible and to feel that we have really used our talents and tastes in our work provides a personal and professional delight that can carry us over the next few rough spots.

So occasionally, the desire to see just how good one of these programs can be does take priority. In the case of *Monkey Face*, the "fine tuning" involved slowing down the elephant anecdote to fit the longer length of that particular flute passage. Also, each segment needed to be timed and rehearsed several times to coordinate with each part of the musical piece. Our preschoolers loved it. An extra bonus came from a father of one of our toddlers who came up after a story hour to say, "That was *really* good."

We were invited to perform *Monkey Face* with the book, puppets, and music at the local North Miami Woman's Club as well. It would be nice if all our presentations could be that well planned and well rehearsed, but when you do these things twice a week, with time and staff shortage pressures always a problem, you tend to simplify whenever possible. Any of five or six other flute pieces on those particular Rampal tapes would have set the tone nearly as effectively, without all the rehearsal and timing efforts.

Of course it is possible to get even more elaborate than I've described. We have, on occasion, used portions of four and five different tapes and records to orchestrate a story. It all depends on how much time one can give to it. Certainly there is nothing wrong with keeping it simple, especially if it is "simple but frequent."

One advantage, however, to doing all the rehearsals necessary to put together a more complex and finished production is that you can more easily repeat it whenever you have a chance to present the program in another place or at another time.

Our invaluable volunteer, Fereydoun, had been able to come to the library to run the movie projector on family film nights. We decided, since we were getting older children at these movies, to try a puppet-and-story presentation for them after the films.

Since I have two daughters—Jeannie and Jill, and Fereydoun has four—Sasha, Annahitta, Odyscea, and Sudey, we had our own built-in troupe of puppeteer-helpers. We even drew crayon portraits of the monkey mother at each stage of her development, and added them to the show.

With a large audience in the evening, a darkened room, the charming flute music of Rampal, and the informal atmosphere of a movie night, the effect was wonderful. One time when the tape was misplaced we did a "regular" version without music, and we could see just how much better it really was with the flute background.

Finally, when our summer children's programs rolled around, we unveiled *Monkey Face* for an elementary-school-age audience. These older, more sophisticated children loved it as much as the pre-schoolers and their parents. It seems that a good story with an imaginative "production" knows no limits in its appeal. The satisfaction derived from being able to come up with enough space, rehearsal time, effort, puppets, and puppeteers was immense.

But coming back to the point about keeping things simple: one can do a solo version of *Monkey Face* with any of those five or six flute pieces playing gently in the background, with no puppets, no puppeteers, no assistants, no props, no lighting effects—and still do a good job. All a librarian, teacher, parent, relative, or babysitter needs is a story, some music, and an audience of one or more. The "Cecil B. De Mille productions" are nice, but the simpler versions are effective too. After all, how many times in this life are you going to have a talented Iranian walk in the door with four children, all of them ready to volunteer to help with children's programs?

Sample Musical Story Hour Program
Theme: Monkeys
Ages: Pre-school and early elementary

1. Participation Game:

You can buy, for a small price, a fuzzy hand-glove with velcro fingertips and plenty of accompanying stick-on characters from a California company:
The Wizard of Ahhs, Inc.
P.O. Box 851
Pollock Pines, California 95726
If you prefer, you can buy a mitt board which fits on your hand, instead of the glove. You can also buy their book, *Monkey Mitt Rhymes*.
Since the story is *Monkey Face*, here is a monkey participation game:

Five Little Monkeys

Five little monkeys jumping on the bed
One fell off and bumped his head
Mama called the doctor,
And the doctor said,
"No more monkeys
Jumping on the bed!"

(Substitute four, three, two, and one in place of five for each following verse.)

2. Participation Game: *Mr. Alligator*

The Wizard of Ahhs's monkeys and alligator can be purchased for this game or puppets can be used. You can make your own monkeys and tape them to your fingers or a handmade glove. You can even make flannelboard characters.

Five little monkeys sitting in a tree,
Teasing Mr. Alligator,
"Can't catch me!"
Then along came Mr. Alligator
Quiet as can be
SNAP, right off the tree

(Substitute four, three, two, and one in place of five for each following verse.)

3. Musical Story

Story:	*Monkey Face*
Music:	"Variations on a Theme by Rossini" (Chopin)
Musical Mood:	The music should be upbeat, light and melodious. This particular selection is also broken up into sections that fit each segment of the story. However, many Rampal flute pieces with a similar light tone make great background music for this story. It is simpler to capture the general tone and mood than to try to orchestrate all the anecdotes in the story. Flute music, in general, goes well with *Monkey Face*.

Puppet Participation:

You need two monkeys, a rabbit, an owl, a crocodile, an elephant, a giraffe, and a lion to do this one with puppets.

4. Weston Woods Filmstrip: *Curious George Rides a Bike*

5. Activity:

   Draw a monkey from the games, or the final "monkey face" from the story. Ten minutes of coloring will give the children a memory to take home.

Other Monkey Stories for Parents and Children to Share at Home (or for Storytelling):

Iwamura, Kazuo. *Tan Tan's Hat*. Bradbury Press, 1978.

Myers, Walter. *Mr. Monkey and the Gotcha Bird*. Delacorte, 1984.

Sutcliffe, Jean. *Jacko and Other Stories*. (McGraw-Hill, 1964).

References

Cassette:

Chopin, Frederic. "Variations on a Theme by Rossini." *The Romantic Flute*. Jean-Pierre Rampal. Everest Record Group MKC-1808.

Book:

Asch, Frank. *Monkey Face*. Parents Magazine Press, 1977.

3.

Matching Music with Characters

Finding music match-ups for Br'er Rabbit, Peter Rabbit, and the Velveteen Rabbit

Now we'll get to the heart of the opportunities I'm talking about. Let's take some actual characters from children's literature and see what musical match-ups can be made, based on the emotional nuances of their individual personalities.

First, here comes Br'er Rabbit, lippitty clippitty down the road, sassy as a jaybird—as Uncle Remus would say. There are no tear-jerking qualities in this rascal as there are in his velveteen relative.

As we follow Br'er Rabbit for a little while we see what he's really like. It appears that Br'er Rabbit went to a Halloween party across the river, and while he was there the wooden bridge collapsed in a storm. Br'er Rabbit has no way to get back home and calls out, "Has anybody got a boat?" His shouts wake up his old nemesis, Br'er Alligator, who slithers over to proffer a friendly ride.

Once into the river, the gator makes his real intentions known, "I'm goin' to goozle out your gizzard!" Thinking fast, Br'er Rabbit explains that he never takes his gizzards (two of them) to a Halloween party; no, he leaves them in a hollow tree across the river. If the gator would take him over there, Br'er Rabbit would show him the tree and let him have both gizzards. When they get to the river bank, off hops Br'er Rabbit, lippitty clippitty, through the woods.

There is no need for any tear-jerking music to portray the personality of Br'er Rabbit. He is a trickster, a survivor—smart, small, fast, witty, full of fun and mischief. What could we use in the way of background music for such a rabbit? Leroy Ander-

17

son has a piece called "Fiddle Faddle" which is fast and funny fiddle music, and it works just fine.

But when we come to Peter Rabbit, we're meeting a different type of personality who requires a little different type of music. Peter has some timidity, fear, and gentleness that bold Br'er Rabbit does not have. We're not looking for solemnity here, but something a little more sensitive than the unbridled, boisterous good humor of "Fiddle Faddle." Anyone familiar with baroque music will remember a very charming piece called Boccherini's Minuet (actually part of his String Quintet in E Major), but many people don't know it, although they may recognize it because it's been transcribed into modern "elevator music" and wafts through many department stores. There is another minuet by Bolzoni which also works well because of the gentle tone and the "hoppity" passages of violin strings. Vivaldi's Concerto in G Major for Two Mandolins and his Concerto in C Major for the Piccolo are easily accessible in any good music store or library collection. They work well with Peter Rabbit, and either of those particular instruments offer the needed combination of smallness, sweetness, and playfulness that seem to suit a little rabbit who is having his troubles in the garden patch.

Turning attention to the Velveteen Rabbit, we find a toy which became real because of the love of the child who owned it. When the doctor announces that the toy rabbit is a mass of scarlet fever germs and must be burned, lumps come to the throats of children and adults alike. The nursery magic fairy, who takes care of toys that children have loved, comes to make the rabbit real, to our great relief. Another tear wells up when the boy meets the real rabbit, never realizing it was his own bunny.

Here we have a real musical challenge. We definitely don't want "Fiddle Faddle" for this story. Yet neither do we want the funereal dirge of Samuel Barber's Adagio for Strings. First of all, the choice will depend on what version of the story is to be used. Will the book be read word for word? Or will it perhaps be retold in a shortened version showing the illustrations? If you are going to hold it to about five or six minutes, consider the quiet but highly emotional baroque favorite, Pachelbel's Canon. Deutsche Grammophon puts out a cassette anthology called *Souvenirs—the World's Most Beautiful Piano Waltzes,* which includes waltzes by Chopin, Brahms, Schumann, Grieg, and Schubert. The general tone of the entire tape goes with the moods of the Velveteen Rabbit and is good background for reading the whole story. Gyorgy Cziffra (and many others) have recorded entire collections of Chopin waltzes and etudes. Robert Schumann's *Kinderszenen (Scenes from Childhood)* is another appropriate piano piece.

Somehow the idea of pairing Chopin with the Velveteen Rabbit appeals to me the most. If you like the idea of Chopin backing up this wistful story, you have found a good excuse to lie on the sofa for several hours listening to the vast number and types of his piano works available. If someone is bugging you to vacuum, fix something, or mow the lawn, tell the pest that you're working!

Here is a list of recommended piano pieces by Frederic Chopin that will go well with this story:

> Ballade no. 3 in A-flat Major
> Polonaise in A-flat Major
> Berceuse op. 57
> Fantasie Impromptu
> Etude in G-flat Major, "Butterfly"
> Etude in G-flat Major, "Black Key"
> Ballade no. 4 in F Minor
> Polonaise in F-sharp Minor
> Three Ecossaises op. 72
> Waltzes nos. 1, 2, 3, 4, 6, 9, 12
> Nocturne no. 17 in B

Phillipe Entremont, Arthur Rubinstein, Guiomar Novaes, and Gyorgy Cziffra are just a few who have fine Chopin recordings, and there are many other good pianists to choose from as well.

I hope this example shows you that it can be great fun matching characters with music. However, a couple of points should be clarified before moving into the wider world of children's literature. One is that you may be inclined to use music which is not classical, and there's nothing wrong with that. You might have a whole collection of Zamfir playing his pan flute, and feel that it sets off your rendition of Peter Rabbit perfectly. Some will even prefer Mantovani. The main reason that classical music is stressed here is for its great range of expression. Classical music is apt to have so much subtlety and shading that the matching possibilities are limitless. I also like the idea of being able to expose children to finely crafted music they may never otherwise hear. This book does lean, then, toward classical music, but there are counterpoints composed of marches, jazz, swing, and novelty music as well. The only kind of music not used is vocal music. It is not practical to tell a story while someone is singing at the same time. The words run together in a jumbled mush. The main idea is that matching characters to music is great fun and the results are dynamite. It is like discovering worlds of wonder that have just not been explored.

Before we leave our rabbits, do you have any ideas for *The Tortoise and the Hare?* How about *Mr. Rabbit and the Lovely Present?* One interesting thing about this book here is that you don't have to use any single match-up used as an example. It is fairly simple to find your own pairings. You can even write a sequel to this book, and suit music to your own episodes.

Moving farther on into the world of children's literature, we'll leave the rabbit patch and venture into the realms of other children's story characters. Some are scarier than rabbits. How about nightmares, monsters, and witches?

Sample Musical Story Hour Program
Theme: Rabbits
Ages: 5–9

1. Participation Game:

The Wizard of Ahhs Co. has five pink and white rabbits which fit on the velcro glove mentioned earlier. Again, if you prefer to make your own or use a flannelboard, be creative!

Five Little Rabbits

Five little rabbits standing by the door
One hopped away, and then there were four

Four little rabbits, sitting near a tree
One hopped away, and then there were three

Three little rabbits, looking at you
One hopped away, and then there were two

Two little rabbits, sleeping in the sun,
One hopped away, and then there was one

One little rabbit, sitting all alone
He hopped away, and then there was none.

2. Filmstrip:

Another excellent Weston Woods filmstrip, *Peter Rabbit*, is a nice change of pace. Turn off all the lights and use a short filmstrip. Children like variety.

3. Participation Game:

Ask for five volunteer children to help with this one.

Five little bunnies came to town,
Came to town,
Came to town.
Five little bunnies came to town.
Hop! Hop! Hop!

(Substitute four, three, and two in place of five to finish the verses. Have one-child bunny hop back into the audience with each verse.)

One little bunny hid in a bush,
Hid in a bush,
Hid in a bush.
One little bunny hid in a bush.
Hop! Hop! Hop!

4. Musical Story:

Story:	"Br'er Rabbit and the Gizzard Eater" (or any similar Br'er Rabbit story)
Music:	"Fiddle Faddle" (Leroy Anderson)
Musical mood:	"Fiddle Faddle" is fast, staccato, peppy, full of fun and humor. Or choose any piece of music which has those qualities to match the personality of Br'er Rabbit. The violins here can be "fiddled" with skitterish speed. You may know some country music records which turn loose the fiddlers.
Puppets:	You need both a rabbit and an alligator for this one.

5. Activity:

Any bunny you can manage to draw and make copies of will do, or perhaps Br'er Rabbit or Peter Rabbit. Coloring these will give the children a lasting reminder of your program. One six-year-old still talks about a program we did two years ago!

References

Cassettes:

Boccherini, Luigi. Minuet. *Boccherini, String Quintet in E Major.* Vanguard/Everyman CSRV 291; and *The Rage of 1710.* Vox/ Turnabout CT–4713.

Chopin, Frederic. *Chopin Waltzes.* Georgy Cziffra, pianist. Philips 411 155–4.

———. *Guiomar Novaes Plays Her Favorite Chopin.* Vanguard C10059.

Pachelbel. Canon. *The Rage of 1710.* Voc/Turnabout CT-4713.

Souvenirs: Beautiful Waltzes for the Piano. Deutsche Grammophon 415 234–4.

Vivaldi, Antonio. Concerto in G Major for Two Violins. *Vivaldi: Concertos for Diverse Instruments.* The Bach Guild CHM 16.

———. Piccolo Concerto in C Major. *Gala Concert in Venice: Music by Antonio Vivaldi.* Duetsche Grammophon 415-233-4.

The World's Favorite Piano Music. Phillipe Entremont, pianist. Columbia/Odyssey YT 35927.

Record Albums:

Anderson, Leroy. "Fiddle Faddle." *Fiddle Faddle.* Arthur Fiedler and the Boston Pops. RCA LM/LSC-2638.

Barber, Samuel. Adagio for Strings. *Romantique.* Carmen Dragon and the Capitol Symphony Orchestra. Capitol P 8542.

Bolzoni. Minuet. *Romantique.* Carmen Dragon and the Capitol Symphony Orchestra. Capitol P 8542.

Chopin, Frederic. *The Chopin I Love.* Arthur Rubinstein, pianist. RCA LSC-4000.

Schumann, Robert. *Kinderszenen (Scenes from Childhood).* Deutsche Grammophon 2531 089.

Books:

Aesop. *The Tortoise and the Hare.* (numerous editions)

Andersen, Hans Christian. *The Little Match Girl.* (numerous editions)

"Br'er Rabbit and the Gizzard Eater." In *Walt Disney's Uncle Remus Stories.* Simon and Schuster, 1946.

Potter, Beatrix. *The Adventures of Peter Rabbit.* Warne, 1903.

Williams, Margery. *The Velveteen Rabbit.* Knopf, 1983.

Zolotow, Charlotte. *Mr. Rabbit and the Lovely Present.* Harper and Row, 1962.

4.

A Little Nightmare Music

Searching for sounds to orchestrate with
Mercer Mayer's nightmare in the
closet—and other folks like him

The little boy tells us that there used to be a nightmare in his closet. One night he decided to wait in bed for it to come out. Sure enough, the nightmare tiptoed across the rug to the foot of the bed. The boy snapped the light on and confronted the monster, shooting it with a toy rifle. The nightmare started to cry. The boy didn't want the nightmare to wake up his parents, so he begged the sobbing monster to hush up. It couldn't stop crying so the boy tucked it into the bed, closed the closet door, and crawled in with the beast. They went to sleep, under the watchful eye of another nightmare peeking out of the closet.

A library aide on our staff who shares our interest in these activities, suggested some Prokofiev to use with this story because of the dissonance and eeriness of some of his music. However, we tried for contrast this time, and used the sleepiest, most peaceful and melodic piece around—Brahms's Lullaby in a rich violin rendition by Carmen Dragon and the Capitol Symphony Orchestra on the album, *Nightfall*. The contrast worked very well indeed, and there were gasps and giggles when the picture of the tiptoeing nightmare appeared, breaking into the previous peace and harmony.

A more recent story, *Too Many Monsters* by Susan Meddaugh, has one unhappy monster living in a forest with other happy monsters who love the darkness and gloom. The Norwegian composer Edvard Grieg knew about the trolls and creatures of his country's folklore. I tried "The Hall of the Mountain

King" from Grieg's *Peer Gynt* Suite for this one, to suit the mood of the monsters. On the other hand, you might want to emphasize a different part of the story, in which our unhappy monster climbs a tree after a pretty butterfly. All the other monsters chase after him, causing the tree to fall, thereby knocking over several other trees. The resulting clearing in the dense forest lets in the sun and creates a place where the monster and his friend the butterfly can live happily and undisturbed.

Suppose you would like to emphasize the butterfly and the lovely patch of sunshine instead of the monsters? Well, in the same *Peer Gynt* Suite you'll find a lyrical section called "Morning Mood." If you want to be clever and impress any musical types among the parents, you could use "Papillons" by Robert Schumann. The odds are about one in a million that anyone will recognize what a clever thing you've done, but you can always tell them at the end of the program!

Let's turn our attention now to a story just about everyone knows—Maurice Sendak's *Where the Wild Things Are*. This is a story that's fun to experiment with. We hold the music until Max's boat comes by to take him across the starlit sea to the land of the wild things. I like to try different pieces of music for this magical boat trip. One favorite is "Over the Waves," or "Sobre las Olas," by the Mexican musician, Juventino Rosas. Carmen Dragon and the Capitol Symphony Orchestra put out an album (*Over the Waves*) with a nice version of this. You may know the tune as "The Loveliest Night of the Year." A couple of other times we tried the slow, majestic parts from the soundtrack of the movie, *Chariots of Fire*. There are parts of Rimsky-Korsakov's *Scheherazade* ("The Sea and Sinbad's Ship") that also work well.

Then, of course, Max comes to the land of the monsters, and a change of musical pace is required, especially when King Max commands his beasts to let the wild rumpus start. This part is really fun to try different pieces of music with. Jascha Heifetz's recording of "Hora Staccato" fits in nicely. There have been times when we used the theme from the movie, *Ghostbusters*—to the delight of the parents and children old enough to recognize the song.

There are also plenty of witches to work with in children's

literature. Take Ida DeLage's *Weeny Witch* and see what kind of musical match we can make. The little girl witch presents an interesting challenge because she does not fit in with the myriad of evil witches around her. First of all, she is just a child. Secondly, while the other witches are determined to capture the Night Fairies who light up the stars every evening, the Weeny Witch feels great empathy for the good fairies. In fact, she lets them loose so they won't die when the sun comes out. Enraged, the older witches go after the Weeny Witch, but she is rescued by the Night Fairies who whisk her off to their queen. Here they discover that the Weeny Witch is their own lost child, stolen as a baby by the witches. The fairies give her a new pair of wings and some beautiful new clothes, to her great happiness.

Richard Wagner's "Ride of the Valkyries" is about as perfect a musical match-up as there is for the wild, scheming witches flying on their brooms and plotting the demise of the good fairies. Music like this can truly capture the character of the witches, their night flights and their wicked ways.

It doesn't, however, fit the ending. The quiet charm of Brahms's Waltz would do nicely, or Offenbach's cheerful "Barcarole" would be a nice ending. There are many pieces to choose from here; for instance, Puccini's *La Bohème* has "Musetta's Waltz" (non-vocal versions are available). Mozart's "Longing for Springtime" ("Sehnsucht nach dem Früling") would also be fine. Schubert's Serenade has a moving, emotional quality, if you wish that much effect, instead of a lighter touch.

Another interesting combination, if you can get the timing rehearsed well, would be the final parts of Beethoven's Symphony no. 6, the "Pastorale" Symphony. There is a terribly violent storm, followed by a calm, bucolic sunny aftermath. There you have one piece that matches the mood of both major sections of the story perfectly. In this case, the story has to be timed just right to coincide with the change in the music.

The use of different selections may be easier to handle. Being able to change the music at any given point gives the flexibility to run long or run short with the telling of the story.

No matter how well rehearsed one may be, something can happen with a live audience to throw off your timing. One boy mashes the fingers of the girl next to him, accidentally, and the resulting shrieks may throw well-laid plans totally out of whack. Be flexible and don't count too much on timing perfection being attainable!

A Sample Musical Story Hour Program
Theme: Monsters and Nightmares

1. Activity: "Itsy Bitsy Spider"

Country Critters Co. has a great spider available to back you up on this. It even squeaks. You can sing this and have the children "climb" with two spidery fingers of their right hand, up their raised left forearm:

The itsy bitsy spider
Went up the water spout.
Down came the rain
And washed the spider out.
Out came the sun
And dried up all the rain,
So the itsy bitsy spider
Went up the spout again.

Since the story is *There's a Nightmare in My Closet*, you can say, "Now we're going to have a story about somebody else who is a little scary—a nightmare who walks out of a closet."

2. Musical Story

Story: *There's a Nightmare In My Closet* (Mercer Mayer)

Music: Brahms's Lullaby

Puppets: Two monsters and a boy (and possibly a toy rifle) are all you need.

| Musical Mood: | The sleepy irony of Brahms's Lullaby contrasts with the spookiness of the nightmare, but you may prefer more eerie music like "In the Hall of the Mountain King" from Grieg's *Peer Gynt* Suite. The Brahms piece is available on many recordings and tapes. |

3. Musical Story:

Story:	*Where the Wild Things Are* (Maurice Sendak)
Music:	"Over the Waves" (Rosas) for nice ocean-going music for Max's trips to and from. Theme from *Ghostbusters* for the Wild Things' dance.
Puppets:	A full cast of Sendak's characters can be purchased commercially.
Musical Moods:	Something to suggest a boat trip is needed. I like "Over the Waves." You could experiment with *Scheherazade* or any other sea-going music as well. *Ghostbusters* theme adds a real touch of humor, besides the rhythm it provides.

4. Activity:

If you can draw and photocopy any make-believe monster or one from your stories, you can give the children a nice tamed, tangible monster they can color and take home with them.

Other Monster Stories for Parents and Children to Share at Home (or for Storytelling):

Demarest, Chris. *Morton and Sidney*. Macmillan, 1987.

Drescher, Henrik. *Simon's Book*. Lothrop, Lee and Shepard, 1983.

Fisk, Nicholas. *Monster Maker*. Macmillan, 1979.

Gackenbach, Dick. *Mag the Magnificent*. Clarion, 1985.

Hutchins, Pat. *The Very Worst Monster*. Greenwillow, 1985.

McCay, William. *Meet My Pet Monster*. Western, 1986.

Mayer, Mercer. *Little Monster at School*. Golden Press, 1978.

Myers, Amy. *I Know a Monster*. Addison-Wesley, 1979.

Nolan, Dennis. *Monster Bubbles: A Counting Book*. Prentice-Hall, 1976.

Parish, Peggy. *Zed and the Monsters*. Doubleday, 1979.

Peck, Richard. *Monster Night at Grandma's*. Viking, 1977.

Sage, Alison. *The Ogre's Banquet*. Doubleday, 1978.

References

Cassettes:

Ghostbusters soundtrack. Arista ACB 6-8418.

Offenbach, Jacques, "Barcarole." *Gaîte Parisienne*. New Philharmonia Orchestra. London/Treasury STS5-15564.

Vangelis. *Chariots of Fire* soundtrack. Polydor CS 825384-4.

Wagner, Richard. "Ride of the Valkyries." *The Ride of the Valkyries: Wagner's Greatest Hits*. Philadelphia Orchestra. CBS/Odyssey YT 38914.

Record Albums:

Beethoven, Ludwig van. Symphony no. 6. Arturo Toscanini and the NBC Symphony Orchestra. RCA Victor LM 1755.

Brahms, Johannes. Lullaby. *Nightfall*. Carmen Dragon and the Capitol Symphony Orchestra. Capitol SP 8575.

Grieg, Edvard. "In the Hall of the Mountain King." *Peer Gynt Suite No. 1*. Columbia ML 6024.

―――. "Morning Mood." *Sibelius: Findlandia, with the Mormon Tabernacle Choir/Grieg: Peer Gynt Suite No. 1/Alfven: Swedish Rhapsody/Sibelius: Valse Triste*. Eugene Ormandy and the Philadelphia Orchestra. Columbia ML 5596.

"Hora Staccato." *60 Years of Music America Loved Best.* Jascha Heifetz, violinist. RCA Victor LM-6074.

Mozart, Wolfgang. "Longing for Springtime" ("Sehnsucht nach dem Frühling"). *The Concert Zither.* Ruth Welcome. Capitol SP 8602.

Puccini, Giacomo. "Musetta's Waltz." *The Concert Zither.* Ruth Welcome. Capitol SP 8602.

Rimsky-Korsakov, Nikolai. *Scheherazade.* London Symphony Orchestra. London PM 55002.

Rosas, Juventino. "Over the Waves." *Over the Waves.* Carmen Dragon and the Capitol Symphony Orchestra. Capitol SP 8547.

Schubert, Franz. Serenade. *The Concert Zither.* Ruth Welcome. Capitol SP 8602.

Books:

DeLage, Ida. *Weeny Witch.* Garrard, 1968.

Mayer, Mercer. *There's a Nightmare in My Closet.* Dial, 1968.

Meddaugh, Susan. *Too Many Monsters.* Houghton Mifflin, 1982.

Sendak, Maurice. *Where the Wild Things Are.* Harper and Row, 1963.

5.

Melodies for Teddy Bears, Real Bears, and Monkeys

Corduroy, Little Bear, and Curious George

Don Freeman's *Corduroy* is a whimsical fantasy with a strong grip on real emotions. What little child hasn't fallen in love with a particular stuffed animal? In a "dream of love," Lisa wishes she could have that special bear, with the button missing—and sure enough, eventually Corduroy becomes hers. To go with this "dream of love," how about the music of the same name—that is, "Liebestraum" no. 3 by Franz Liszt? There are various versions—piano or orchestral—by many different artists. This particular piece has the slow pace, the depth of emotion, the ability to move an audience, and the tenderness that match the heart-tugging warmth in *Corduroy*.

Another piece with a long-lasting emotional impact is Massanet's Meditation (from *Thais*.) I remember the first time I heard this slow, extremely moving music. I'd been dating a ballet dancer in college and she talked me into going to see two ballet dancers perform. The lights went down, the audience grew still, the stage suddenly had two blue spotlights on Melissa Hayden and Jacques D'Amboise dancing to a violin solo rendition of the Massanet piece. It still lingers in my mind, even though a couple of decades have slipped by.

There are plenty of slow, emotionless pieces of music, but for a story like *Corduroy* I prefer music that can move people, unforgettable music, to go with the moving and unforgettable story.

A third musical piece with that haunting quality is Handel's Largo from *Xerxes*. All three are hypnotic and mesmerizing, and they add something special.

Just as you could make a case for a similarity between Corduroy and the Velveteen Rabbit—and their musical choices could be interchangeable—you could also make a case for the similar emotional tone of Little Bear and Peter Rabbit. Charming, small, overcoming problems, not supercharged with heavy action or heavy emotion.

Let's take a good look now at Elsa Minarik's Little Bear, using *A Kiss for Little Bear*. Our young hero draws a picture and asks his friend the hen to take it to Grandmother. She is so thrilled with the picture from her grandson that she gives the hen a kiss to take back to him. On the way to deliver the kiss, the hen stops off and gives it to the frog to deliver, instead. The frog gives it to the cat and goes swimming in the pond. The cat gives it to the skunk, who tries to give it to the pretty girl skunk to deliver. She gives it back. He returns it to her. This goes on and on until the hen protests and delivers it herself. Little Bear tries to get her to deliver another kiss to Grandmother, but she refuses on the grounds that these things just get too complicated. The skunks, by the way, get married, and Little Bear is the best man.

Sometimes you can find an anthology of music whose title is a tip-off to the type of music inside. *Romantique,* from the Capitol Symphony Orchestra, is obviously a collection of romantic pieces that might go with this romantic tale of Little Bear's skunk friends. If you listen to an entire theme album like this, you may turn up several good choices. In this case, Anton Rubinstein's Melody in F stood out. Rubinstein, a protégé of Liszt and a teacher of Tchaikovsky, wrote in an unabashedly romantic, elegant, and sophisticated style. The lyricism of this particular piece fits the story well.

Rudolph Friml's "L'amour Toujours L'amour" is another choice from the album. The sprightly, dance-like yet dignified "Giga" by Corelli, also on the album, illustrates how well these theme albums can give you a number of choices.

Curious George! Just mention the name and the anticipation level zooms. What a challenge—and a delightful one—to look for music to match this monkey's antics. I suppose part of the appeal of George is that children identify with a hero so curious about everything, like themselves, that he can find more ways to get himself in trouble than anyone could imagine. And yet, of course, he always means well! He certainly didn't know the zoo's ostrich would swallow the trumpet George offered. He didn't know that pulling the lever in the dumptruck would cause it to dump sand all over the lady in the flowered hat. He couldn't think ahead enough to realize the huge snowball he rolled down the hill would knock the skiers and sledders for a loop. When he tried to feed the rare fish to the seals at the aquarium he thought he was doing a good deed. When he tried to dial a phone number, he was merely imitating his friend, the man in the yellow hat, not trying to start a panic in the fire department or land in jail for the false alarm. I suppose every parent could tell similar stories about their children, leaving no doubt about the realistic appeal of Curious George. After a great deal of experimenting, I've found several pieces of music that are appropriate for our very special monkey friend. The opening movement of Mozart's *Eine Kleine Nachtmusik (A Little Night Music)* is about perfect. It's also easily found in music stores and library collections because it's a "standard." The peppiness, mischievousness, and good humor match George and add even more charm to him, if that's possible.

I would like to go off the deep end a little here. Mostly we've stayed with "standards" because chamber music is *not* easily accessible and I don't want to give the impression that the musical ideas in this book are either inaccessible or difficult to use. Nevertheless, Mozart has some gorgeous chamber music which some of you may be able to locate. The Concerto in C for Flute and Harp may be one of the loveliest things you'll ever hear, and the same emotional symbiosis with the character is present. The playfulness and charm of the flute and harp interacting are especially appropriate in stories where George is directly involved with another character, such as the scene where he is bouncing from seal to seal in the water tanks of *Curious George Goes to the Aquarium.*

Between Mozart's first concerto (for piano, K 175) and his last (the clarinet concerto) there were 447 pieces in eighteen years. The chamber music available from this period is full of works for horns, flutes, violas, violins, harps, bassoons, oboes, and clarinets. This music on recordings may not be readily available at local record stores, but most can look up listings and labels in Schwann's catalog and order from the producing company's distributor (see references). If you have access to much of Mozart's chamber music, (personal or library collections) by all means, experiment on your own.

Sample Musical Story Hour Program
Theme: Bears
Ages: 4–8

1. Song: The Bear Went over the Mountain

The bear went over the mountain
The bear went over the mountain
The bear went over the mountain
To see what he could see

(And what did the bear see?)

The other side of the mountain
The other side of the mountain
The other side of the mountain
Was all that he could see

2. Participation Game:

The Wizard of Ahhs sells five velcro-backed bears to stick on the velcro-finger glove. You could use these, or create your own, or use flannelboard figures. The children can hold up the correct number of fingers for each verse, and call out the number of bears left:

Five Little Bears

Five little bears dancing on the floor,
One fell down, and then there were four.
Four little bears climbing up a tree,
One found a beehive, and then there were three.
Three little bears, wondering what to do,
One went for a swim, and then there were two.
Two little bears looking for some fun,
One chased a rabbit, and then there was one.
One little bear, missing all his brothers,
Wished upon a star, and ran home to Mother.

3. Musical Story:

Story: *Corduroy*

Music: Meditation from *Thais* (Massanet)

Musical Mood: This story requires music with an emotional, heart-tugging quality. You could also experiment with the theme from Schubert's Unfinished Symphony and any similar pieces.

Puppets: A bear, a girl, a woman sales clerk, a store guard, a mother, depending on available materials.

4. Filmstrip:

Weston Woods' *Little Bear's Visit*

5. Activity:

Coloring. A bear going over a mountain or a character from your story or filmstrip—whatever you can draw, with plenty of large, white open spaces, photocopied for each child to color and keep.

Other Books that Parents and Children can Share Together (or for Storytelling).

Asch, Frank. *Happy Birthday, Moon.* Prentice-Hall, 1982.

Bassett, Lisa. *Beany and Scamp.* Dodd, Mead, 1987.

Berenstain, Stan. *The Berenstain Bears and the Messy Room.* Random House, 1983.

Boon, Emilie. *Belinda's Balloon.* Knopf, 1985.

Calhoun, Mary. *The Night the Monster Came.* William Morrow, 1982.

Carlstrom, Nancy. *Jesse Bear, What Will You Wear?* Macmillan, 1986.

Dalgliesh, Alice. *The Bears on Hemlock Mountain.* Charles Scribner's Sons, 1985.

Degen, Bruce. *Jamberry*. Harper and Row, 1983.

Gage, Wilson. *Cully Cully and the Bear*. Greenwillow, 1983.

Gretz, Susanna. *Teddy Bears Stay Indoors*. Four Winds Press, 1987.

Hill, Eric. *Baby Bear's Bedtime*. Random House, 1984.

Jonas, Ann. *Two Bear Cubs*. Greenwillow, 1982.

Mack, Stan. *10 Bears in My Bed: A Goodnight Countdown*. Pantheon, 1974.

Minarik, Else. *Little Bear's Friend*. Harper and Row, 1960.

Pryor, Bonnie. *Grandpa Bear*. Morrow, 1985.

Vincent, Gabrielle. *Ernest and Celestine's Picnic*. Greenwillow, 1982.

References

Cassettes:

Handel, George Frederick. Largo from *Xerxes*. *The Rage of 1710*. Vox/Turnabout CT 4713.

Mozart, Wolfgang. *Eine Kleine Nachtmusik*. *Albinoni: Adagio/Pachelbel: Canon/Mozart: Eine Kleine Nachtmusik and More*. Toulouse Chamber Orchestra. Seraphim/XDR 4XG-60271.

Record Albums:

Corelli, Arcangelo. "Giga." *Romantique*. Carmen Dragon and the Capitol Symphony Orchestra. Capitol P8542.

Friml, Rudolph. "L'amour Toujours L'amour." *Romantique*. Carmen Dragon and the Capitol Symphony Orchestra. Capitol P8542.

Liszt, Franz. "Liebestraum" no. 3. *Liebestraum: Favorite Melodies of Liszt*. Columbia ML 6123.

Massanet, Jules. "Meditation" from *Thais*. *Great Music for Relaxation*. RCA Victor LSC-2800.

Mozart, Wolfgang. Concerto in C for Flute and Harp. *Mozart: Music for Winds and Brass.* Murray Hill S-4364.

Rubinstein, Anton. Melody in F. *Romantique.* Carmen Dragon and the Capitol Symphony Orchestra. Capitol P8542.

Books:

Freeman, Don. *Corduroy.* Puffin Books, 1968.

Minarik, Elsa. *A Kiss for Little Bear.* Harper and Row, 1968.

Rey, H. A. *Curious George.* Houghton Mifflin, 1941.

———. *Curious George Rides a Bike.* Houghton Mifflin, 1952.

Rey, Margaret. *Curious George and the Dump Truck.* Houghton Mifflin, 1984.

———. *Curious George Goes to the Aquarium.* Houghton Mifflin, 1984.

———. *Curious George Goes Sledding.* Houghton Mifflin, 1984.

6.

Slithery Snake Music

(and some thoughts on Spencer Shaw's 1950s Brooklyn Programs)

Elaine Gordon, our local representative in the Florida legislature, contributed $35 to our library so that we could buy a twelve-foot-long stuffed boa constrictor for our children's programs. This was one of the items we had listed on our Friends of the Library "wish list." It's rather a humorous-looking boa, so it's not likely to scare any small children. One of the main reasons for putting the snake on the list was to be able to do a spectacular version of *Crictor*.

This particular boa curls around me with no need to be held, its head resting on top of my shoulder, peering out at the audience while I tell the story from Tomi Ungerer's book. When Madame Bodot, Crictor's owner, takes the snake along to help her teach school, then my twelve-foot snake becomes a real source of delight for the children in my audience. I bend Crictor into a "B," a "D," an "M," a "W," a "C," and a "G" to illustrate how he teaches the little students their letters. Then he bends into numerals, like an "8," or "6," or a "3."

After this, I give one end of the snake to one of my adult volunteers, while I hold the other. Then we ask a young volunteer to come forward from the audience, so we can demonstrate how Crictor let the schoolchildren use him as a jump rope. This always gets a big reaction.

Another audience-participation opportunity comes at the end of the story. One of the children can come forward with the medal to hang around Crictor's neck, after the snake coiled himself around the robber who had tried to rob Mme. Bodot's apartment.

Now let's see what we might use in the way of slithery snake music to go with this story. First we'll look at specific instruments which might suggest a snake—the clarinet and the flute.

Mozart's Clarinet Concerto, in its opening and closing movements, seems to give a feeling that fits the animal's movement and his personality as well. Mozart has a clarinet quintet which also would fill in well, if you avoid the adagio movement. Crictor is too full of pep for a low, somber adagio piece. This second famous clarinet piece—the Quintet in A major for Clarinet and Strings—has a first and fourth movement which work well.

Jean-Pierre Rampal has recorded any number of flute pieces which could be used. He has a cassette tape called *Flute and Guitar—an 18th Century Serenade* which he recorded with guitarist Rene Bartoli. Any section of Giuliani's Grand Sonata in A Major for Flute and Guitar from this recording blends well with Crictor.

Mozart himself wrote two flute pieces which are also perfect for Crictor. The Flute Concerto no. 1 in G and the Flute Concerto no. 2 in D are equally effective. You could pick which movements you wish to use depending on the pace at which you want to tell the story on any particular day.

One of the advantages of having a coiled twelve-foot boa constrictor that clings is that I can take it along with me on school visits. Since the kids are not used to seeing their teachers with stuffed snakes, the appearance of a guest speaker with a coiled boa around him commands, instant attention. For example, I can use the story to get elementary school students to sign up for the more elaborate productions at the summer library program. If there happens to be a convenient outlet in a classroom, I can also use a tape of the music.

An advantage to having the snake donated by a state representative, by the way, is that it makes for natural publicity and even lends itself to photographs. I write for our city's employee newsletter and have had library articles appear in professional library publications and local newspapers. Any publicity that we can generate from a program helps create a greater awareness of what we are doing.

I began to wonder, as I paired clarinets and flutes with a snake, if other musical instruments would be "naturals" for other animals or characters. The line from the opening of Walt Disney's animated version of Prokofiev's *Peter and the Wolf* came to mind. While the narrator explains which musical instruments represent which characters, he says, "Grandpapa is an old bassoon." The boy, Peter, is represented by sprightly violins. The menacing wolf's presence is always preceded by the glowering French horns. The cat is a low clarinet. The duck is an oboe. The hunters are kettle drums and a bass drum, and the flighty little bird is a flute.

The idea for matching music with characters or stories is not new for films and music such as *Peter and the Wolf*. You may recall the classic pairings Disney used in *Fantasia*. Yet the idea has not been used very frequently in public library storytelling. Spencer Shaw, however, was mastering the technique in Brooklyn when he wrote an article called "Recorded Magic for Story Hours" for the October 1958 issue of *Top of the News*.

Mr. Shaw spoke of using the beautiful Spanish folk tune, "La Golondrina" (the swallow) in combination with Leo Politi's *Song of the Swallows*. He also identified another pairing which struck me as even more inspired—using "Ave Maria" with *The Juggler of Notre Dame*. I felt real excitement when I found Spencer Shaw's thirty-year-old article on the subject. He asked questions of his own programming: Do they inspire? Do they educate? I surely would have loved to hear Spencer Shaw in front of "Ave Maria," telling a story! It had to be an inspirational and unforgettable experience. He also wrote about using candle lights, spot lights, curtains, and other dramatic effects.

I must say that I was encouraged in my own efforts, both at programming and writing, to see that a man of Spencer Shaw's caliber and renown had also felt that music, lighting, and other effects could add something rich and special to storytelling.

A Sample Musical Story Hour Program
Theme: Dinosaurs, Monsters, and Snakes
Ages: Pre-school and early elementary

1. Participation Game (fingergame or flannelboard, with the children calling out the numbers):

Five Fat Funny Dinosaurs

Five fat funny dinosaurs
   Letting out a roar.
One went away, and then there were four.
Four fat funny dinosaurs
   Munching on a tree.
One went away, and then there were three.
Three fat funny dinosaurs
   Didn't know what to do.
One went away, and then there were two
Two fat funny dinosaurs
   Having lots of fun
One went away, and then there were none.
One fat funny dinosaur
   Afraid to be a hero.
He went away, and then there were zero.

2. Musical Story

Story: *Crictor* (by Ungerer)

Music: Clarinet Concerto, First Movement (Mozart)

Musical   Slithery like a snake, yet upbeat like Crictor.
Mood: Clarinet music seems a good match.

3. Stuffed Animal Involvement:

A stuffed snake (try your zoo's gift shop if you can't find one in another store) can be bent into the letters and numbers into which Crictor is bent to teach the schoolchildren in the story. After the story you could ask your group if they would like you to try to make other letters or numbers with the snake.

4. Jump-Rope Snake:

You can invite the children to play jump rope with you and an assistant each holding an end of Crictor, very low to the ground, swinging the snake back and forth slowly.

5. Coloring Activity:

Any long silly snake you can draw and reproduce is fun to color. You might even do a triceratops or some other elaborate dinosaur for coloring. It depends upon how artistic you are!

References

Cassette:

Giuliani, Mauro. Grand Sonata in A Major for Flute and Guitar. *Flute and Guitar—an 18th Century Serenade.* Jean-Pierre Rampal, Rene Bartoli. Columbia/Odyssey YT-60218.

Record Albums:

Mozart, Wolfgang. Clarinet Concerto. *Mozart—Music for Winds and Brass.* Murray Hill S-4364.

———. Flute Concerto no. 1 in G. *Mozart—Music for Winds and Brass.* Murray Hill S-4364.

———. Flute Concerto no. 2 in D. *Mozart—Music for Winds and Brass.* Murray Hill S-4364.

———. Quintet in A Major for Clarinet and Strings. *Mozart—Music for Winds and Brass.* Murray Hill S-4364.

Prokofiev, Sergei. *Peter and the Wolf.* Cyril Ritchard, narrator. Columbia MS-6027.

Book:

Ungerer, Tomi. *Crictor.* Harper and Row, 1958.

Article:

Shaw, Spencer. "Recorded Magic for Story Hours." *Top of the News,* October 1958.

7.

Tall Tales

Copland and Grofé meet Pecos Bill and a few other heroes

Now we will search for authentic American music to use in combination with some authentic American tall tales.

We might as well go right into Texas to start, and see what we can do for Pecos Bill. Here's someone who can lick a pack of coyotes, tame the wildest of wild horses, bust a cyclone, invent a lariat—and even handle wild women. This latter, you may recall, was no easy job, even for the likes of Pecos Bill. He enlisted the help of his bucking bronco, Widow Maker, for this one. Sweet Sue disobeyed Bill, as usual, and tried to ride his horse. Widow Maker bucked her so high, she finally came down and went into a perpetual bounce. Only when Sweet Sue promised to obey Bill did he get out his lariat and lasso the bouncing girl.

Aaron Copland's *Rodeo* is a good choice to use with Pecos Bill. The exuberant, multi-tempo Western melodies of this modern classic make a perfect background for the hyperbolic heroics of this larger-than-life Texan. *Billy the Kid* is another Copland piece that fits right in. The Boston Pops has an album *(The Pops Goes West)* with a great rendition of "Deep in the Heart of Texas" which also is appropriate and appealing.

By contrast, Johnny Appleseed stories are less frenetic in their tone and pace. Searching for a musical mood for this planter of trees calls for a differently paced approach. We find that "On the Trail," from Ferde Grofé's *Grand Canyon Suite* adds a nice touch to the stories. The pace is steady and leisurely, just as I picture Johnny Appleseed's steady pace while planting the seeds in so many locations.

Paul Bunyan and John Henry are the two American folk heroes most connected with the business of getting work done. For all his size and muscle, Paul put his mind to inventing things, too—the grindstone and the two-man saw, for instance.

Much of the humor in Paul's stories is tongue-in-cheek. For example, when infant Paul was in his cradle out at sea, just kicking his feet caused huge waves and flooding. For a musical background, a quieter Western piece allows the humor to wend its way into the audience's consciousness without too much commotion. "San Antonio Rose" sets the tone well, without intruding upon the humor in Paul's accomplishments.

John Henry's story, however, has a strong element of pathos, which requires a similar tone to make a musical match. John Henry's race against the machine results in his own death. The dignified and moving strains of "Shenandoah" add a nice touch to the finale of John Henry's story.

Windwagon Smith, of course, needs no such dignified music. Here's a fellow with a great idea of sailing by land to the West. Trouble is, such a wild ride isn't too easy on the stomachs of the usual landlubbers who become interested enough to try the wild, windy voyage. An instrumental version of "Don't Fence Me In" sets a nice tone for this type of story, not so wild that it distracts from the humor of the events in the storytelling.

Then there's Davy Crockett, soldier, congressman, and comet licker. The Crocketts were not ordinary people, of course. Even Davy's ma could jump a seven-rail fence backwards, dance a hole through a wooden floor, cut down a gum tree ten feet in diameter, and sail across the river, using her apron for a sail. Davy's wife, Sally Ann Thunder Arm Whirlwind Crockett, could blow out the moonlight and sing a wolf to sleep. Davy's children, likewise, could out-scream any creature in creation and out-fight a thunderstorm. Davy himself could catch and tame a bear—Death Hug by name.

This hero appears to call forth a romping type of music, without the need for subtlety that Paul Bunyan suggests. The theme from the old television series, "Bonanza," is as good a Western romp as any.

Going from land to sea, we look for some orchestration for a sea-going down-East Yankee, Captain Alfred Bulltop Stormalong. When he was only thirteen, Stormy signed on as a ship's cabin boy. Adventure befell him quite soon as a ten-tentacled Kraken monster grabbed hold of the ship from underneath, trapping it in his grasp. No one knew what to do, so Stormalong dove into the water and began "wrassling" with the beast. The worried crew was happy to see him come up again. He explained to them that he tied a different type of sailor's knot in each of the Kraken's ten tentacles!

Later on, as the heroic sailor matured, he fought the British with John Paul Jones. Eventually he got his own clipper ship, taking cargoes to India, China, and Russia. Finally, he became a whaler, able to hurl harpoons five times as far as the normal man.

A musical change of pace from all the previous American heroes is required here. "Columbia, the Gem of the Ocean," "Blow the Man Down," or some of Rimsky-Korsakov's *Scheherazade* ("The Sea and Sinbad's Ship") are all good background for Stormalong's tales.

It is interesting to think about what type of music would be most effective with individual interpretations of these American hero tales. All of us would not approach them in the same way. We prefer the uninhibited romp music for Pecos Bill and Davy Crockett; a toned-down romp for the less boisterous Windwagon Smith; a quieter background approach for the mighty Paul Bunyan; and a dignified emotional background for John Henry; sea music for Stormalong. Other people might prefer entirely different musical moods. Orchestrating the American heroes is certainly a challenge and there are plenty of wide open spaces for experimentation and debate!

A Sample Musical Story Hour Program
Theme: Tall Tales
Ages: 5–9

1. Musical Story:

Story: Any Pecos Bill story

Music: *Rodeo* (Copland) (many versions available)

Musical   Wild cowboy music
Mood:

2. Musical Story:

Story: Any Davy Crockett story

Music: "Bonanza" theme

Musical   Robust and western
Mood:

3. Musical Story:

Story: Any Stormalong tale

Music: "The Sea and Sinbad's Ship" (Rimsky-Korsakov)
            (many versions available).

Musical   Music which suggests the sea.
Mood:

4. Activity:

Coloring any one of the three folk heroes would give the
children fun and a memory to take home.

References

Record Albums:

"Bonanza" theme. *The Pops Goes West*. Arthur Fiedler and the
    Boston Pops. RCA Victor LSC-3008.

"Columbia, the Gem of the Ocean." *Over the Waves*. Carmen
    Dragon and the Capitol Symphony Orchestra. Capitol SP
    8547.

Copland, Aaron. *Billy the Kid*. CBS MG 30071.

———. *Rodeo*. CBS MG 30071.

"Deep in the Heart of Texas." *The Pops Goes West*. Arthur Fiedler and the Boston Pops. RCA Victor LSC 3008.

"Don't Fence Me In." *The Pops Goes West*. Arthur Fiedler and the Boston Pops. RCA Victor LSC 3008.

Grofé, Ferde. "On the Trail." *The Grand Canyon Suite*. Capitol SP 8347.

Rimsky-Korsakov, Nikolai. "The Sea and Sinbad's Ship." *Scheherazade*. London PM 55002.

"San Antonio Rose." *The Pops Goes West*. Arthur Fiedler and the Boston Pops. RCA Victor LSC-3008.

"Shenandoah." *The Pops Goes West*. Arthur Fiedler and the Boston Pops. RCA Victor LSC-3008.

Book:

Blair, Walter. *Tall Tale America*. Coward McCann, 1944.

8.

The Sea

Debussy, Ravel, and Strauss can add watery images to Swimmy and other dwellers of the deep

The lush and watery colors that Leo Lionni uses for his book *Swimmy* lend a tone of mystery, the unknown, and fear, for surely fear is a major factor in this story. The little red fish are eaten by a large tuna early in the tale, and only the little black fish, Swimmy, escapes. Fear is intensified as other predators swim by—the tentacled jellyfish, the eerie eel, the clawed lobster. Lionni's use of purples and blues, blacks and greens, deepens the sense of lurking danger.

Swimmy is able to join another school of small red fish, but they are scared to swim openly because of the predators. The tiny black fish comes up with the idea of all the red fish banding together in the shape of one large fish, with himself as the "eye." The idea works and they are left alone by the larger fish.

The sea has many moods, and so the music for such stories will be likewise varied. Perhaps for Lionni's story the mood could best be suggested by Ravel's *Daphnis and Chloe* no. 2. The mysterious passages in Debussy's *La Mer* are also appropriate. Another good choice, perhaps better for younger children because it has less "turbulence," is "The Aquarium" from Camille Saint-Saens' *Carnival of the Animals*. This latter captures the mystery and unknown quality, without the stormy or dangerous undertones that are present in the other two pieces. Choices, therefore, depend on the ages and sensitivities of your audience, and your own judgment.

We can try the sea in an entirely different mood, returning to our friend Harry the dirty dog for his excursion to the ocean.

Harry by the Sea, by Gene Zion, is a cheerful, funny book. The colors are predominantly orange and yellow, and the mood is sunny. It's so sunny in the story, in fact, that poor Harry tries to escape from the heat by finding some shade. He goes under the family's beach umbrella, but is chased away because of lack of room. He crawls into the children's sand castle, but is yelled at for breaking it apart. He follows a fat lady, who casts a big shadow, but is yelled at again for annoying her.

Down to the water goes Harry, where he is knocked head over heels and strewn with seaweed, a terrifying sight for the bathers, who think Harry is a sea monster. After inadvertently terrorizing the whole beach full of bathers, Harry loses the seaweed and is recognized by his family again. They promptly put up a large enough beach umbrella for Harry to sit under in the shade with them.

For such a "terror," unlike the real life-threatening terror Swimmy faces, a musical background needs to be free of any scary elements. I've had my best luck using the cheery and flowing Johann Strauss popular classic, the "Blue Danube Waltz." There is usually an appreciative chuckle from the parents and, at the same time, a mood of good-natured, watery background for the children enjoying the story.

My only problem with this story was in trying to use real seaweed with a puppet. After awhile, the seaweed smelled so it couldn't be kept. We substituted some clumps of dead grass and weeds that served the purpose with only a slight loss of authenticity.

Indeed, the sea has many moods. For an entirely different type of story, try Mark Taylor's book, *Bobby Shafto's Gone to Sea*, based on the song of the same title. Our hero is fat with yellow hair, a ladies' man but not a man's man. Pretty Bobby Shafto's father told him he must give up singing love songs and go to sea to become a man.

Bobby didn't want to go, and his sweetheart (Susan Gray) didn't want him to go either. The crew of the ship *Delight* also wished that useless, nauseous Bobby had stayed home. They finally try him as a cook, but his stew is so awful, the crew nearly dies.

When pirates capture the ship, however, Bobby's true worth

becomes apparent and his talent the critical factor in the salvation of the crew. His singing thrills the pirates' ladies, so Bobby's mates are kept alive as long as this continues. Then Bobby offers to cook his stew for the pirates! They become so sick to their stomachs that Bobby's crew takes over the ship and Bobby sails back into port as a hero.

For this story, I like an instrumental version of "Blow the Man Down," which Carmen Dragon arranged for the Capitol Symphony Orchestra. There are also instrumental versions available on both children's and adult records of sea ditties like "Sailing, Sailing" and "The Hornpipe Dance" which work well. The children's album *Singing Games* has both of these in instrumental versions despite the title.

Such merry music could also be used with poems of the sea. William Cole put together a collection of poems, songs, and stories in his anthology, *The Sea, Ships and Sailors*.

I like to use the poem, "I Saw a Ship a'Sailing," which describes the crew of 24 white mice and the duck captain. "And when the ship began to move, the captain cried, 'Quack! Quack!' " "Captain Pink of the Peppermint" is another favorite from this collection. It is about how the long-suffering crew of the *Peppermint* finally got fed up with the nasty old captain, who groused through a crack in his jaw rather than waste his breath by yelling at them. They unceremoniously dumped him overboard and sailed off in the opposite direction.

Another boisterous sea yarn, taking its place among American tall tales, is Robert McCloskey's *Burt Dow, Deep Water Man*. As of this writing, this story is twenty-five years old—and as fresh as it was a quarter century ago. Burt Dow, retired deep water man, still keeps a leaky old boat, the *Tidely Idley*, for a little fishing off the New England coast. This is a whale of a tale all right, for Burt hooks a tail of a whale. Eventually Burt talks to the whale, removes the hook and applies a band-aid to the little wound. As all this transpires, a storm comes up unnoticed. Burt asks the whale to temporarily swallow the boat, Burt himself, and his pet seagull to keep them safe from the storm. The whale complies, but once inside, Burt and the gull began to worry that the whale didn't understand English and wouldn't "unswallow" them. Burt's recipe to upset the whale's stomach includes bilge water, rusty fish hooks, yellow deck-paint, grease, and then tickling the whale's throat with a feather. A whale of a burp sets Burt free. All the other whales, however, surround him until he puts band-aids on their tails, too!

For this romp of a sea story I use a piece of music which suits the mood perfectly—although the title does *not* fit: "The Skaters' Waltz" by Emil Waldteuful (1837–1915), pianist to Empress Eugenie of France and musical director of the court balls. Older kids (and any adults present) might recognize the piece as "The Skaters' Waltz" and wonder what that has to do with a sea story, so the recognizable title would only detract. I use it therefore only with preschool audiences (who don't know a *thing* about Empress Eugenie or Waldteuful or his only famous title out of 250 pieces!). They just know the music goes nicely with that story.

Stories and poems of the sea reflect many moods, and finding the appropriate type of music to go with each mood can be a real challenge. Frightening, mysterious, cheerful, light, or humorous—it is an interesting search for combinations. I *could* say that you really have to keep your head above water for this type of work!

A Sample Musical Story Hour Program
Theme: The Sea
Ages: 4–8

1. Participation Game: Finger Game

> There are so many fish
> In the deep blue sea.
> What color fish does ＿＿＿ see? (insert child's name in the blank)
> (Put a different colored fish on each finger one at a time.)
> (From *Mitt Magic, Fingerplays for Finger Puppets.* Gryphon House, 1985.)

2. Participation Game: Finger Game

Use the Wizard of Ahhs velcro glove and stick on frogs or your own creations:

Five Little Speckled Frogs

Five little speckled frogs
Sitting on a speckled log,
Eating some most delicious bugs,
"Yum! Yum!"

One jumped into the pool
Where it was nice and cool.
Now there are just four speckled frogs,
"Glub, glub!"

(Substitute four, three, two, and one in place of five to finish each verse.)

3. Musical Story:

Story:	*Harry by the Sea* (Gene Zion)
Music:	"Blue Danube Waltz" (J. Strauss)
Musical Mood:	Watery, light, and cheerful
Puppets:	A dog, a boy and a girl, a beach guard, a hot dog man, a fat lady. If you can find an umbrella that passes for a beach umbrella and make a cardboard box into a sand castle, that would serve you very well.

4. Musical Story:

Story:	*Swimmy* (Leo Lionni)
Music:	"The Aquarium" from *Carnival of the Animals* (Saint-Saens)
Musical Mood:	Watery and mysterious, somewhat eerie

5. Participation Song:

"Row, Row, Row Your Boat"

6. Activity:

Coloring. Take your choice of one fish, a school of fish, one or five frogs, or characters from your stories. The children love to color something you've just presented and take it home.

References

Cassette:

Saint-Saens, Camille. "The Aquarium." *Carnival of the Animals.* Seraphim 4XG-60214.

Record Albums:

"Blow the Man Down." *Over the Waves.* Carmen Dragon and the Capitol Symphony Orchestra. Capitol SP 8547.

Debussy, Claude, "La Mer" ("The Sea"). *Afternoon of a Faun, Daphnis and Chloe no. 2, and La Mer.* Eugene Ormandy and the Philadelphia Orchestra. Columbia ML 5397.

"Hornpipe Dance." *Singing Games.* Merry Children's Records MR 6005.

Ravel, Maurice. "Daphnis and Chloe" no. 2. *Afternoon of a Faun, Daphnis and Chloe no. 2 and La Mer.* Eugene Ormandy and the Philadelphia Orchestra. Columbia ML 5397.

"Sailing, Sailing." *Singing Games.* Merry Children's Records MR 6005.

Strauss, Johann. "The Blue Danube." *Strauss Waltzes.* Westminster XWN 18500.

Waldteuful. "The Skaters Waltz." *Arturo Toscanini and the NBC*

Symphony Orchestra—Nutcracker Suite, Skaters Waltz, and Others. RCA Victor LM 1986.

Books:

Cole, William (editor). *The Sea, Ships and Sailors*. Viking, 1967.

Lionni, Leo. *Swimmy*. Pantheon, 1963.

McCloskey, Robert. *Burt Dow, Deep Water Man*. Viking, 1963.

Taylor, Mark. *Bobby Shafto's Gone to Sea*. Golden Gate Junior Books, 1970.

Zion, Gene. *Harry by the Sea*. Harper and Row, 1965.

9.

Speed and Action

Stories and music that make hearts beat a little faster

Let us turn our attention to a type of book which whooshes along with great gusto and speed. Trying to find music that can keep pace with a story like *Harriet and the Roller Coaster* can be a lot of fun in itself.

Nancy Carlson's schoolmate friends, George (a rabbit) and Harriet (a dog) look forward to spending their last day of Lassie Lower School at the class visit to the amusement park. George taunts Harriet that she'll be too chicken to ride the roller coaster. "It goes so fast that if you don't hold on you'll fall right out," he assures her. Harriet bravely replies that she will ride the roller coaster and show George that she is not chicken. Nevertheless, she doesn't sleep too well that night.

The big day comes and there is much anticipation as they look at the awesome, intimidating roller coaster. George and Harriet get on board and off they go.

It works well to hold the music until precisely this point of the story and then suddenly start "The Flight of the Bumblebee." The unexpected arrival of Rimsky-Korsakov's exciting music at that moment adds a real punch to the story. Also, the fact that the frenetic piece only lasts just over a minute makes it suitable for just a part of the story rather than the whole. There are many renditions of this piece available, but I use James Pappoutsakis's flute version, which was recorded with Arthur Fiedler and the Boston Pops. It doesn't matter much which version you choose.

By the time the music and the wild ride end, I get back to my unaccompanied telling of the ending. Harriet loved the ride, but George is sick. He has to sit down on a bench while Harriet continues on her merry way, going back to ride the roller coaster again. No music is needed here, as the boastful, crestfallen George watches the girl happily ride away. You can't find a more delightful and perfect match-up of music and story than this one.

A similarly paced story, in which the action suddenly takes off, is *Nutty's Birthday* by Claire Schumacher. In this story, Nutty the Squirrel's birthday party is taking place in the same park as the party of a little boy named Tom. Nutty's father tells his son to climb up into the tree to find his present. Meanwhile Tom has received a model airplane for *his* birthday present, and promptly flies it. Of course, the airplane gets stuck in the same tree in which Nutty is looking for his own present, so he hops in. Someone pulls the string to get the plane unstuck, and off it flies—with Nutty in it.

As in the story of *Harriet and the Roller Coaster*, this is the ideal moment to start the music. Use Jascha Heifetz's violin version of "Hora Staccato" for the wild plane ride. Again, there are many equally peppy versions of the piece available. Another piece, which adds a touch of genuine surprise and humor at this moment, is the famous "Can Can" from Offenbach's *Gaité Parisienne*. This is the type of musical surprise that elicits squeals of delight from youngsters and their parents as well.

"The Gingerbread Man" is another story in which speed is an integral part of the plot. Once the cookie in question gets clear of the confines of the oven, he must run away from the old woman, the old man, the cow, the horse, and the cat before being conned into the fox's mouth.

Once again, the music need not start until the action really heats up. Here is a good chance to use Chopin's "Minute" Waltz (which takes roughly two minutes, despite the title). This sprightly piece takes just enough time to get the galloping cookie away from all his pursuers, and leave a silence for his encounter with the fox.

This would be an opportune time to look at some other types of music besides classical. Boots Randolph, the jazz saxophone player, has his famous "Yakety Sax" piece, which is perfect for humorous chase scenes. The English comedian Benny Hill uses it a lot for his many filmed chases.

The dixieland classic "That's a' Plenty" is also ideal. If you can't recall the tune, try to remember the music that struck up on the old Jackie Gleason shows when the rotund comedian hoisted his leg and shouted, "And away we go!" When Gleason called to Ray Bloch and his orchestra, "A little travellin' music please," the band played "That's a' Plenty."

You will think of many more stories involving speed. One of my favorites is Jean Horton Berg's *Miss Tessie Tate.* Unlike the other speed stories, the action here begins on page one as Tessie roller skates past the women who spend their time in more domestic pursuits like cleaning the house and washing clothes. All day and night this liberated lady skates.

It looked as though she would come to a bad end for her eccentric, sporting ways. However, the king has a problem with his castle, and Tessie is the only person who is able to help him solve it. The castle is so big that it takes fifty maids to keep up with the cleaning. The overcrowding meant that the king and queen and their children have very little room to move around. Also, the staff seems to be eating up all the food in the castle. The king offers ten bags of gold and "one elegant pearl" to any sharp-witted woman who can clean the castle by herself. Tessie, with her roller skates, swoops and swirls, does figure-eight's, with a duster in one hand and a broom in the other, cleaning the entire castle to perfection. Besides winning the gold and the pearl, Tessie also wins a permanent job cleaning the castle twice per week.

For this story, there are many appropriate musical selections. One is the finale from Von Suppe's *Light Cavalry* Overture. Another is "the Lone Ranger part" from Rossini's *William Tell* Overture. Almost any overture from these two composers has parts which would fit Tessie's activities.

The Boston Pops's album, *Holiday for Strings,* has a couple of excellent choices. One is the title piece, and the other is Hayman's "No Strings Attached." Depending on your pace for telling the story, you could use either alone or combine the two for a more leisurely telling.

At any rate, you can see the terrific possibilities of matching

some delightfully fast-paced stories with some equally delightful musical romps.

A Sample Musical Story Hour Program
Theme: Speed and Action
Ages: Pre-school and early elementary

1. Participation Game: Squirrels

The speaker and the children rise up from the floor, sit down
on the floor, and rise halfway up at each mention of up,
down, and halfway up.)

There were lots of squirrels
Some were boys and some were girls
And they climbed up the tree
And they climbed down the tree
And when they're up, they're up
And when they're down, they're down
But when they're only halfway up
They're neither up nor down.

2. Musical Story:

Story: *Nutty's Birthday* (Claire Schumacher)

Music: "Hora Staccato"

Musical   Fast, surprising, exciting to go with the squirrel's
Mood: wild plane ride

3. Participation Game:

The Wizard of Ahhs velcro-tipped glove and five stick-on
bees are good for this.

Beehive

Here is the beehive
Where are the bees?

They're hidden inside
Where nobody sees
Soon they come creeping
Out of the hive
One . . .
Two . . .
Three . . .
Four . . .
Five . . .
Bzzzzzzzzzzzzzzz

3. Musical Story:

Story:	*Harriet and the Roller coaster* (Nancy Carlson)
Music:	"Flight of the Bumblebee" (Rimsky-Korsakov)
Musical Mood:	Fast, surprising, action-packed
Puppets:	You need a dog (Harriet), a rabbit (George), and a cut-out poster-board roller coaster if you want puppets to act out behind you as you tell the story.

5. Activity:

Coloring. Draw a bee, a squirrel, or a character from your story. Photocopy it and let each child color.

References

Cassette:

Rossini, Gioacchino. *William Tell* Overture. *Rossini—William Tell and Other Overtures.* Philips Classette 411 163-4.

Record Albums:

Chopin, Frederic. "Minute" Waltz (Waltz in D-flat, opus 64, no. 1). *The World's Favorite Chopin.* Arthur Rubinstein, pianist. RCA LSC-3322.

Hayman, Richard. "No Strings Attached." *Holiday for Strings.* Arthur Fiedler and the Boston Pops. RCA Victor LSC-2885.

"Hora Staccato." *60 Years of Music America Loves Best.* Jascha Heifetz, violinist. RCA Victory LM-6074.

Offenbach, Jacques. "Can Can." *The Lure of France.* Columbia CS 8111.

Rimsky-Korsakov, Nikolai. "The Flight of the Bumble Bee." *Holiday for Strings.* Arthur Fiedler and the Boston Pops. RCA Victor LSC-2885.

Rose, David. "Holiday for Strings." *Holiday for Strings.* Arthur Fiedler and the Boston Pops. RCA Victor LSC-2885.

That's a' Plenty." *At the Jazz Band Ball.* The Dukes of Dixieland. Vik LX-1025.

Von Suppe, Franz. *Light Cavalry* Overture. *Hi Fi Hits in Popular Classics. Volume 2.* Westminster XWN 18724.

"Yakety Sax." *Boots Randolph's Yakety Sax.* Monument SLP 18002.

Books:

Berg, Jean Horton. *Miss Tessie Tate.* Westminster Press, 1967.

Carlson, Nancy. *Harriet and the Roller Coaster.* Carolrhoda, 1982.

The Gingerbread Man. Whitman, 1958.

Schumacher, Claire. *Nutty's Birthday.* Morrow, 1986.

10.

Spooks, Witches, and Goblins

Wagner, Dukas, and Mussorgsky can cast an eerie spell over Halloween and ghost stories

One of the more delightful challenges of matching music with stories involves the "spooky, scary stuff," as the kids say.

Let's work in reverse for a change, and start with a piece of music, then look for a story to go with it. When I first heard *Carnival of the Animals,* a piece for two pianos and orchestra by Camille Saint-Saens, I noticed particularly a part called "Fossils." A lecture by Leonard Bernstein on another tape explained how the composer was trying to give a musical representation of bones, and succeeded in this comical musical section.

By chance one day I found the perfect book to go along with the music, *Funnybones* by Allan and Janet Ahlberg. This particular combination of music and story is perfect. The large skeleton, small skeleton, and their pet dog skeleton leave their dark cellar one night to go for a walk. They throw a stick for the dog to fetch, but when he jumps for it, he collapses into a pile of bones. The music sounds like clattering bones throughout. They try to put the dog back together but they put its head on backwards. They can tell because the dog says "Foow" instead of "Woof." They finally get it right, cheerfully singing, "the hip bone's connected to the leg bone," etc., while they assemble the dog.

The three then go to the zoo and ride the elephant bones, talk to the talking bird bones, and shy away from the crocodile bones. On their way home, they look for someone to scare. Finding no one else, the silly trio decides to scare each other, before returning to their home in the cellar.

Carnival of the Animals also provides some excellent passages for lions, turtles, swans, elephants, and birds. I will return to it in a later chapter.

I began reflecting on my own childhood experiences with music one day, trying to dredge up recollections of what music I was exposed to as a child. The first thing that came to mind was the unforgettable background music to the fabulous *Flash Gordon* movie serial shown each week on early television. Buster Crabbe was the young, blond hero of this thriller that no kid in our Philadelphia neighborhood would miss. How could any of us deny the thrill of the evil Emperor Ming trying to conquer the universe? Or Flash's beautiful girlfriend, Dale Arden? Or their scientist friend, Dr. Zharkov? But above all, there was the music! The choice of that music was inspired. I did not know what it was, but many years later, I found it: *Les Preludes* by Franz Liszt. That music really is everything Flash Gordon was to us—exciting, powerful, triumphant, pure adventure.

Once again I started with the music and looked for a story, one that had all the mystery and excitement of the evil Ming and the feel of the unknown in the universe! The story is *Tailypo—a Ghost Story* by Joanna Galdone (Illustrated by Paul Galdone).

An old man lives alone in a cabin with three dogs, Uno, Ino, and Cumptico-Calico, in the middle of the deep woods. They are surrounded by tall, spooky trees. While the old man is dozing off, a mysterious creature with a long furry tail slips through a crack in the logs of the wall. Racing after it with a hatchet, the old man chops off the creature's tail.

The old man falls asleep that night only to be terrorized by a noise—scratch, scratch, scratch—like a cat's clawing. "Tailypo," the voice moans. All the voice wants is its tailypo. (You can tell that this story lends itself to a hammy telling, sound effects, and wild music!) The dramatic tension of the story builds throughout the night as the voice continues to visit the shivering old man. The creature leads the dogs off to the swamp, and they never return. It's just the man and the un- known beast left—and pretty soon it's only the beast.

You can tell that story a couple of ways, and switch music accordingly. Liszt does nicely with an uninhibited and loud version. However, you could also tell this story in a small, whispery, hushed voice with an intimate tone. You could drag it out slowly with much anticipation. In the latter case, the fireworks of *Les Preludes* won't serve very well at all. No matter how slowly you tell the story, the events are still agitating and frightening. I therefore rule out a very slow, calm piece of music in favor of something quieter than Liszt, but still agitated in mood. The third movement of Beethoven's *Moonlight* Sonata (not the best known movement), played rather low, sets the mood well. The first movement of his *Appassionata* Sonata does just as well.

Let's turn our attention now toward a mysterious cat with bright green eyes. Natalie Savage Carlson's black cat, in *Spooky Night*, shows up one night on the welcome mat of Mrs. Bascomb who is just returning from a P.T.A. meeting. When she finds the cat at her front door, she befriends it and takes it in. It seems to be a gentle and affectionate cat and the family adopts it.

Not until the last day of October does the cat start acting strangely. At this point, things start to happen and so the music is held until now. I'm after some exciting witches-and-demon music here. Camille Saint-Saens, in a mood different from that of *Carnival of the Animals,* works well for this one. His *Dance Macabre* has conjured up witches ever since he wrote it in 1874. Saint-Saens, by the way, was a great admirer of Liszt and greatly influenced by him. Liszt's symphonic poem form encouraged Saint-Saens to try the genre four times, including this piece.

Back to the story, it turns out that the witch who owned the cat, Spooky, comes back for him, but Spooky wants to stay with the Bascombs and become a contented lap cat. The witch wants to play with the full moon, but her flying broom handle is broken, so if Spooky will catch the moon for her, she will grant the cat's wish. Spooky, swept up by the wind, steps from star to star and lands on the moon, sinking it toward earth. Since he is able to get the moon for the witch, he is free. The Bascomb kids have no idea what adventures Spooky has been through, but they do notice his paws are covered with golden specks!

Not all Halloween stories are fanciful or otherworldly. Carol Carrick wrote one called *Old Mother Witch* that has a real psychological twist. Two boys, David and Scottie, hate and fear the cranky old woman, Mrs. Oliver, who lives alone in the old, creaky house. "Old Mother Witch," they call her. They draw a picture of the old hag (with a wart on her nose) on her sidewalk. They decide to ring Mrs. Oliver's doorbell. Mrs. Oliver is having a genuine heart attack and coarsely mumbles, "Help me." The boys run for help, and probably save her life. Later in the story, Mrs. Oliver, recovered, comes knocking at David's door. He is afraid to answer. He waits until she is gone, then goes out to the fence, where the grateful old woman has left some chocolate chip cookies and a note saying only, "Thank you."

Music for a "witch" story of this kind requires something thoughtful and sentimental with a good deal of feeling. Perhaps the theme music from Schubert's *Unfinished* Symphony would be about the best music for such a story. It is an emotional piece for a story of human relationships.

Ian Serralier's book, *Suppose You Met a Witch*, presents us with the type of witch young David had in mind at Mrs. Oliver's. In rhythmical, poetic prose, Serralier introduces us to two more children, Roland and Miranda, who meet the real thing in the person of Grimblegrum the witch. "I'll gobble you yet," she keeps threatening. The children think they have drowned the witch at Ten Foot Bridge the previous summer, but she keeps coming back to get them. She does indeed capture them, but Miranda springs for the magic wand and pinches it up from the evil witch's pocket. They drown the witch again, but she reappears. More complications ensue, but after many convolutions of plot, the children escape and a cowman burns the witch.

This one requires some pretty wild and witchy music to go with it. I can recommend either Mussorgsky's *Night on Bald Mountain* (or *Bare Mountain*, depending on the translation), or Wagner's *Ride of the Valkyries*. Both have the spirit, the spookiness, and the wildness that add the proper flavor to the story.

Now let's meet another witch, one who has to work hard to be as mean as she thinks she ought to be. Don Freeman's *Tilly Witch* stands high atop her mountain admiring the lovely, moonlit night. It makes her feel like being kind to everyone in the world, especially children. She turns into such a nice witch that when she tries to turn back to normal, she can't.

Tilly puts on her purple dress and grabs her flying surfboard. Off she flies, on a desperate journey to the island of Wahoo where Doctor Weegee will tell her how to become a real witch again.

For the airborne surfboard ride, the silence can be broken with Khachaturian's "Sabre Dance." The wild, pulsating staccato rhythms and robust chords of this piece have saved it from the obscurity of the *Gayne Ballet* music it comes from. "Sabre Dance" is the only part of that ballet which has become a popular classic.

Dr. Weegee tells Tilly to fly directly to Miss Fitch's Finishing School for Witches. As she mounts the flying surfboard again, bring back Aram Khachaturian for an encore. Miss Fitch is exasperated with Tilly's niceness, although Tilly shrieks at one point, "I'm the Queen of Halloween, and I have important duties to attend to."

Once graduated, Tilly mounts her surfboard, once again to the wild rhythms of "Sabre Dance," and flies off to scare children everywhere on Halloween night. One more encore of "Sabre Dance," only this time turn the volume knob slowly down as Tilly flies off farther and farther into the night.

You may suspect from reading this section that the "Halloween Puppet and Story Spectacular" is my favorite library event (the Valentine's Day Special runs a close second). Getting a chance to match composers like Liszt, Wagner, Beethoven, Mussorgsky, Saint-Saens, and Khachaturian to children's stories is great fun.

It is also fun to invite the children and their parents to come dressed in their Halloween costumes. The event takes on a festive air and everyone enjoys seeing the other costumes as well as hearing the stories. If you give out treats at such an event, be sure someone on your staff stands by the bowl or table, to ration out the goodies fairly. There is a tendency for some of the faster and more aggressive kids to grab the most they can get in their hands and clean the place out!

A Sample Musical Story Hour Program
Theme: Halloween
Ages: Pre-school and early elementary

1. ## Participation Game:

    The Wizard of Ahhs velcro-tipped glove and four stick-on pumpkins (and one witch) are good for this:

    ### Halloween

    Four little pumpkins
    Sitting on a fence
    A witch came riding by
    Ha Ha Ha! I'll take you home
    And make a pumpkin pie

    (Substitute three, two, and one as you continue the verses. Ask children how many are left each time.)

2. ## Finger Game, Glove Game, or Flannelboard Game:

    ### Five Little Pumpkins

    Five little pumpkins, sitting on a gate.
    The first one said, "My it's getting late."
    The second said, "There's wind in the air."
    The third said, "But we don't care."
    The fourth said, "It's Halloween fun!"

    "Woo-oo-oo-oo!" went the wind
    And out went the lights.
    These five little pumpkins
    Rolled out of sight.

3. ## Musical Story:

    Story: *Tilly Witch* by Don Freeman
    Music: "Sabre Dance" (Khachaturian)

Musical
Mood: Wild, frantic, exciting

4. Musical Story:

Story: *Funnybones* (Allan and Janet Ahlberg)

Music: "Fossils" from *Carnival of the Animals* (Camille Saint-Saens)

Musical
Mood: Spooky, evocative of bones, yet humorous

5. Activity:

Coloring a witch, pumpkins, or even a skeleton would be ideal.

Other Halloween Stories for Parents and Children to Share at Home (or for Storytelling)

Bunting, Eve. *Scary, Scary Halloween.* Clarion, 1986.

Carlson, Nancy. *Harriet's Halloween Candy. Carolrhoda, 1982.*

Feczko, Kathy. *Halloween Party.* Troll, 1985.

Gantos, Jack. *Rotten Ralph's Rotten Trick.* Houghton Mifflin, 1986.

Guthrie, Donna. *The Witch Who Lives Down the Hall.* Harcourt Brace Jovanovich, 1985.

Hautzig, Deborah. *Little Witch's Big Night.* Random House, 1984.

Kelley, True. *The Mouse's Terrible Halloween.* Lothrop, Lee and Shepard, 1980.

Kroll, Steven. *The Biggest Pumpkin Ever.* Holiday House, 1984.

Mueller, Virginia. *A Halloween Mask for Monster.* Albert Whitman, 1986.

Prager, Annabelle. *The Spooky Halloween Party.* Pantheon, 1981.

Rockwell, Anne. *A Bear, a Bobcat and Three Ghosts.* MacMillan, 1977.

Rose, David. *It Hardly Seems Like Halloween.* Lothrop; Lee and Shepard, 1983.

Segal, Joyce. *The Scariest Witch in Wellington Towers.* Coward, McCann and Geoghegan, 1981.

Titherington, Jeanne. *Pumpkin, Pumpkin.* Greenwillow, 1986.

Wiseman, Bernard. *Halloween With Moris and Boris.* Dodd, Mead, 1975.

References

Cassettes:

Saint-Saens, Camille. "Fossils." *Carnival of the Animals.* Seraphim 4XG-60214.

Wagner, Richard. "Ride of the Valkyries." *Ride of the Valkyries: Wagner's Greatest Hits.* CBS/Odyssey YT 38914.

Record Albums:

Beethoven, Ludwig van. Sonata no. 14 in C-sharp (*Moonlight* Sonata). *Beethoven—Three Favorite Sonatas.* Rudolph Serkin, pianist. Columbia MS 6481.

———. Sonata no. 23 in F Minor *(Appassionata). Beethoven—Three Favorite Sonatas.* Rudolph Serkin, pianist. Columbia MS 6481.

Khachaturian, Aram. "Sabre Dance." *Hi Fi Hits in Popular Classics. Volume 1.* Westminster XWN-18888.

Liszt, Franz. *Les Preludes. Great Men of Music—Franz Liszt.* Time-Life STL-567.

Mussorgsky, Modest. *Night on Bare Mountain. The Power of the Orchestra.* Royal Philharmonic Orchestra. RCA Victor VCS-2659.

Saint-Saens. *Danse Macabre. Hi Fi Hits in Popular Classics. Volume 2.* Vienna State Opera Orchestra. Westminster XWN-18724.

Schubert, Franz. Symphony no. 8 (*Unfinished* Symphony). Seraphim SLP 8034.

Books:

Ahlberg, Allan and Jane. *Funnybones.* Greenwillow, 1980.

Carlson, Natalie Savage. *Spooky Night.* Lothrop, Lee and Shepard, 1982.

Carrick, Carol. *Old Mother Witch.* Seabury Press, 1975.

Freeman, Don. *Tilly Witch.* Puffin Books, 1969.

Galdone, Joanna. *Tailypo, a Ghost Story.* Seabury Press, 1977.

Serralier, Ian. *Suppose You Met a Witch.* Little, Brown, 1973.

11.

Valentine's Day Programs

Sweet melodies for lovey-dovey stories

My second favorite program at the library each year (after the Halloween show) is the Valentine's Day Story Hour and Puppet Show.

A wonderful book to use for storytelling is *The Valentines Bears* by Eve Bunting. There is a box full of hand puppet bears and other donated stuffed bears (enough to change the players many times over) in our library which can be used in the puppet stage while the story is being told.

Mrs. Bear has never spent a Valentine's Day with Mr. Bear because, of course, bears hibernate all winter long. She carefully prepares for the day she will wake up her sleeping husband. Mrs. Bear gathers up dried bugs and other treats for a mid-winter picnic, and creates a couple of Valentine's cards with personalized messages ("Termites are sweet and so are you").

She has trouble rousing her mate who pretends to be still asleep. Mrs. Bear gets some ice water from the river to pour on him, but he jovially jumps up and the ice water spills all over her instead. Undaunted, the romantic pair settle down to have themselves a perfectly lovely picnic.

The album *The Romantic Zither*, featuring Ruth Welcome on the zither, offers many soft selections that make nice background music for the story: "Love is a Many Splendored Thing," "Red Sails in the Sunset," "Embraceable You," and "True Love" are just some of the tunes that fit the mood of the story well.

If you would like to get more creative than this, you might want to try the really romantic second movement of Rachmaninoff's Piano Concerto number 2. This slow "adagio sostenuto" is described in the album notes as "a hazy, half slumbering melody . . . briefly stirred up as though a wind storm had blown through . . . and soon returning to the original quietly singing mood."

When you examine the story of *The Valentines Bears*, you will notice the same emotional pattern, and with a little practice you can coordinate a perfect match here.

The Rachmaninoff piece, in this second movement, is basically an alternating duo between the piano and the violins. It captures the sleepiness, the cold winter, and the romantic mood of the bears all at once.

It is interesting to note the background of the piece, dedicated to a Dr. Dahl. It seems Rachmaninoff's first symphony had been considered a failure in Moscow and the composer went into seclusion and a deep depression, writing practically nothing for a period of two years. He finally sought the help of a physician, Dr. Dahl. After three months of daily treatment, including auto-suggestion psychology, Rachmaninoff recovered and wrote this second piano concerto. The piece was completed in 1901 and became one of his two most popular and enduring works.

From this brief look at the background of the work, it is easy to see why the piece comes across as brimming with feeling and emotion. It marked the emergence of the composer from despair into triumph.

And now, a venture into a particularly exciting kind of music to use with a story. Since we're talking about Valentine's Day, we turn to one of the most romantic types of classical music in the world—Spanish guitar music.

This discovery came when we invited a local young classical guitarist, Vance Koenig, to perform in our library. His singer wife, Midori Matsui, came along for some vocals with guitar accompaniment. At that time, before our expansion project gave our library a new wing, we held lectures and film showings in the library itself as opposed to a separate auditorium. We had never tried it with a musician.

Vance was a young fellow, trying to establish himself, and he was used to performing in noisy restaurant-lounges where most people rarely even glanced at him.

He didn't seem to mind when someone started noisily dumping dimes and nickels into the nearby copy machine. We hadn't thought about the copy machine, but thankfully the user was finished soon. It is not often that one hears such a talented musician playing such gorgeous pieces, and I made a special effort to get the names of the music Vance had played.

Within the year I found a record for sale which contained several of those pieces. Guitarist Narciso Yepes's *La Guitarra Española* was an album sitting on a shelf in a local record store with a red sale sticker, "$2.99" on it. Like Vance Koenig, this album was not used to being looked at or paid much attention to. While the Led Zeppelin and other rock records or tapes were selling for $8.95, $9.95, or $10.95, here was a musical treasure for $2.99.

Let's take what is possibly the all-time romantic children's story for this Valentine's program—*Cinderella*. I especially like Paul Galdone's version since the illustrations are so good and so visible from a distance. Galdone's caricatures of the two haughty stepsisters are particularly "snooty" with their overly long noses.

Goodness is rewarded—at least in this story. The fairy godmother changes a pumpkin into a carriage, mice into horses, lizards into footmen, a rat into a coachman, and Cinderella's rags into finery, complete with glass slippers. Off she goes to the prince's ball, hurriedly running out at midnight, losing her slipper. The prince's search for the matching foot, of course, leads him to Cinderella.

What a wonderful story for Spanish guitar music! The works of Tarrega are particularly steeped in lyricism and romance. "Recuerdos de la Alhambra" ("Memories of the Alhambra") is especially haunting and fitting. Another piece, which runs about twice as long (eight minutes, fifty seconds) is the "Gran Jota." Either of these pieces makes a terrific match with our rags-to-riches heroine.

Edward Lear's *The Owl and the Pussycat* is another romantic tale you can use in a Valentine's program. It is also another excellent story for Spanish guitar music, since the owl "sings to a small guitar" about his love for the cat as the two sail the sea in their beautiful pea-green boat. The romantic pair are eventually married by the pig in the woods, who supplies the wedding ring by removing the ring in his nose. The happy couple dance joyously in the light of the moon.

A small guitar and the rocking seas are very well conjured by the unforgettable guitar piece, "Asturias" by Albeniz. It's truly an exciting pairing, and I hope some of you are able to experiment with using Spanish guitar music with romantic stories.

Valentine's programs need not be without rollicking humor. Jak Prelutsky's collection of humorous poetry, *It's Valentine's Day*, contains such efforts as "I Love You More than Apple Sauce," "I Made My Dog a Valentine," and "Jelly Jill Loves Weasel Will." The poems are cute and full of the forthright humor children respond to.

This calls for something lighter and less serious sounding in the background. Perhaps you could experiment with the "Pizzicato Polka" of Johann Strauss, Jr. and Josef Strauss. Another nice choice is "Liebesfreud" by Fritz Kreisler. Yet another, Lumbye's Concert Polka for Two Violins, can be found on the same album as these other two: the Boston Pops's *Holiday for Strings*.

If you don't mind going from the sublime to ridiculous in this chapter, there is a very silly but crowd-pleasing record you can squeeze in. Someone donated to our library an old album of Tiny Tim's falsetto and ukelele music, including "Tip Toe Through the Tulips With Me" and "Ever Since You Told Me That You Love Me (I'm a Nut)." These may never rank up there with Rachmaninoff, but with two puppets and some cardboard tulips, they are side-splittingly funny. Don't try to use a story with Tiny Tim—he has to go it alone!

A Sample Musical Story Hour Program
Theme: Valentine's Day
Ages: Pre-school and early elementary

1. Participation Game:

From the Wizard of Ahhs's *Monkey Mitt Rhymes:*

Five Valentines

Five valentines from the ten-cent store.
I sent one to mother, now there are four.
Four valentines, pretty ones to see.
I gave one to brother, now there are three.
Three valentines, yellow, red and blue.
I gave one to sister, now there are two.
Two valentines, my we have fun!
I gave one to Daddy, now there is one.
One valentine, the story is almost done.
I gave it to baby, now there are none.

(The kids can call out the numbers, if you pause).

2. Musical Story:

Story:	*The Valentines Bears* (Eve Bunting)
Music:	Piano Concerto no. 2, second movement (Rachmaninoff)
Musical Mood:	Romantic
Puppets:	You would just need two bears and a pillow if you want puppets behind you and the book.

3. Musical Story:

Story:	*The Owl and the Pussycat* (Edward Lear)
Music:	"Asturias" (Albeniz)
Musical Mood:	Romantic
Puppets:	One owl, one cat, a boat, a turkey, and a pig.

4. Activity:

Coloring—lots of hearts, or your own version of the owl and pussycat in their boat.

Other Valentine's Stories for Parents and Children to Share at Home (or for Storytelling)

Bennett, Marian. *My First Valentine's Day Book*. Children's Press, 1985.

Devlin, Wende. *Cranberry Valentine*. Macmillan, 1986.

Modell, Frank. *One Zillion Valentines*. Greenwillow, 1981.

Ross, Dave.*Little Mouse's Valentine*. Morrow, 1986.

Sharmat, Marjorie. *The Best Valentine in the World*. Holiday, 1982.

Whitehead, Pat. *Best Valentine Book: ABC Adventure*. Troll, 1985.

References

Record Albums:

Albeniz, Isaac. "Asturias." *La Guitarra Española*. Narciso Yepes, guitarist. Everest 3274.

"Embraceable You." *The Romantic Zither*. Ruth Welcome. Capitol ST 1527.

"Ever Since You Told Me That You Love Me (I'm a Nut)." *God Bless Tiny Tim*. Reprise/Warner Brothers 6292.

Kreisler, Fritz. "Liebesfreud." *Holiday for Strings*. Arthur Fiedler and the Boston Pops. RCA Victor LSC-2885.

"Love is a Many Splendored Thing." *The Romantic Zither*. Ruth Welcome. Capitol ST 1527.

Lumbye. Concert Polka for Two Violins. *Holiday for Strings*. Arthur Fiedler and the Boston Pops. RCA Victor LSC-2885.

Rachmaninoff, Sergei. Piano Concerto no. 2. Svjatoslav Richter, pianist. Deutsche Grammophon 138076.

"Red Sails in the Sunset." *The Romantic Zither*. Ruth Welcome. Capitol ST 1527.

Strauss, Johann. "Pizzicato Polka." *Holiday for Strings*. Arthur Fiedler and the Boston Pops. RCA Victor LSC-2885.

Tarrega. "Gran Jota." *La Guitarra Española*. Narciso Yepes, guitarist. Everest 3274.

————. "Recuerdos de la Alhambra." *La Guitarra Española*. Narciso Yepes, guitarist. Everest 3274.

"Tip Toe Through the Tulips with Me." *God Bless Tiny Tim*. Reprise/Warner Brothers 6292.

"True Love." *The Romantic Zither*. Ruth Welcome. Capitol ST 1527.

Books:

Bunting, Eve. *The Valentines Bears*. Clarion, 1983.

Galdone, Paul. *Cinderella*. McGraw-Hill, 1978.

Lear, Edward. *The Owl and the Pussycat*. (numerous editions)

Prelutsky, Jack. *It's Valentine's Day*. Greenwillow, 1983.

12.

Other Special Days

Hanukkah, Thanksgiving, Easter, Washington's Birthday, The Fourth of July, Christmas

As Christmas approached one year, the telephone rang and a woman identified herself as Barbara Samuels from Temple Beth Moshe. She requested a time in mid-December to bring forty children for a storytime or puppet show. "We'd like a Hanukkah story," she explained. "Not a Christmas story."

We hadn't had a Hanukkah story here before, so I had to scramble to come up with something. A story by Sholom Aleichem called *Hanukkah Money* seemed just right. It seemed like a story the children would enjoy, about two little boys who were terrifically excited about getting holiday money from their father, Uncle Bennie, Uncle Moishe Aaron, and other relatives. The boys were not very concerned with their prayers, candles, and other serious religious activities. They thought mostly of the presents they were due to get.

I played quite a few selections from a recording of Jewish tunes, before I found something I thought I could use. The instrumental album was called *The Soul of Israel*, by the 101 Strings. "Exodus" was certainly too heavy and serious to use with my lighthearted story. Several others posed the same problem.

Finally I found "Tzena, Tzena, Tzena," and I thought this was perfect. However, I didn't know what the translation of "Tzena, Tzena, Tzena" was, and I didn't want to use anything that might somehow offend anyone. Barbara Samuels didn't know. She asked everybody at Temple Beth Moshe, and they didn't know either. I asked our Jewish reference librarian. She had never heard of the word or the song, nor had one of our older volunteers. All of them agreed that the song must be okay, and that if it weren't, nobody would know the difference anyhow!

More than a year later, as this book was going to press, I learned from someone who speaks fluent Hebrew that "Tzena, Tzena, Tzena" is an Israeli folk song from the 1950s. Its translation ("Go out, go out, go out, young women/And see the soldiers in the village./Don't be afraid and hide . . .") may not match the story, but the Israeli sound and cheerful humor of the tune do.

My favorite story for Thanksgiving is Janice's *Little Bear's Thanksgiving*. This has to be one of the most charming holiday stories ever written. There isn't a lot of action, and there is a purely quiet charm to the story. Little Bear's friend Goldie, a young blonde child, invites him to come for Thanksgiving dinner. Little Bear would truly like to go, but he knows he'll be asleep, hibernating, when the day comes.

Some of his friends—a squirrel, a bird, and an owl—agree to wake Little Bear up on the big day. Sure enough, the squirrel drops a nut on Little Bear's head, waking him up in time to go. The friends accompany Little Bear to Goldie's house, and she promptly invites them all in for Thanksgiving dinner. All the animals sit around the table, complete with two long festive candles.

The music needed for this story would also be quiet and unobstrusive. I chose "September Song" in an instrumental version by Ruth Welcome on the zither from the album, *Sentimental Zither*. Although the lyrics aren't present, they fit ("and these few precious days, I'll spend with you . . .") The slow, quiet, emotional rendition of this piece makes an excellent background for the Thanksgiving story.

Let us look at another special holiday—Easter. One of my favorite stories for Easter is Carol Carrick's picture book, *A Rabbit for Easter*. Her husband, Donald Carrick, did the pictures and the two work very well together in telling this realistic story.

Young kindergarten student Paul loves to feed raisins to Sam the rabbit in school. The teacher always reminds the children to return Sam to his cage and lock him in so the rabbit does not wander away and get lost.

Paul is very happy to be chosen to take the rabbit home and care for it over the Easter vacation. He chases his cat Fluffy away from the cage and watches over the rabbit closely.

All is well until Paul is distracted by Stacey, one of his friends, calling him out to see her new two-wheel bicycle with training wheels. When Paul goes outside, he forgets to lock the rabbit back in its cage. When Paul returns, the rabbit is missing.

Paul searches the house, with no luck. Then he frantically searches for the cat, and locks it out of the house when he finds Fluffy asleep on an outdoor garbage can. The boy enlists the aid of his mother in the continued search for the rabbit. The most realistic part of the story has Paul pleading, "Oh, Sam, where are you?" Sam, of course, pays no attention.

Musically it seemed that a gentle piece involving the interplay of two instruments would best reflect the interplay of Sam and the rabbit. I found several pieces on a tape called *Flute and Guitar—an 18th Century Serenade,* on which Jean-Pierre Rampal teamed up his flute with Rene Bartoli's guitar to create some gorgeous music. Jean-Baptiste Loellet's Sonata in A Minor for Flute and Guitar is a slow, gentle duo. Mauro Giuliani's Grand Sonata for Flute and Guitar is a bit more on the peppy side. Depending on your preference, either makes a fine accompaniment.

In a book called *Holiday Puppets* by Laura Ross, there is an interesting story for a Washington's Birthday (or Presidents' Day) program called "Washington and the First Flight in America." It calls for band music as Monsieur Blanchard shakes hands with President Washington before the Frenchman departs on the first balloon trip in America. Washington gives the adventurer a letter, saying he hopes Blanchard won't have to use it.

Blanchard flies from Philadelphia to New Jersey, but is accosted by a startled farmer with a rifle upon landing. The illiterate farmer can't read the words of George Washington, telling all Americans to welcome Blanchard, but he can recognize the presidential seal. All ends well thanks to President Washington's foresight.

Since this story calls for band music, it is especially appropriate to use a good John Philip Sousa march with the story, like "The Gladiator," or "El Capitan," or "Stars and Stripes Forever," all of which conjure up images of Washington.

Once, near the Fourth of July, I used a string of six consecutive Sousa marches to back up a "Patriotic Puppet Parade" in which dozens of flag-carrying puppets marched across our nine-foot stage to the patriotic music. One hundred and twenty-five people clapped and cheered with the *very* loud musical parade.

Several years ago I discovered some conferences that struck me as being far more creative than any I had been to before. They were regional meetings of the Puppeteers of America. At one conference in Tampa, I had the good fortune to meet and hear Eleanor Boylan, at the auditorium of the University of South Florida, where Mrs. Boylan performed her one-woman shows of Aesop's fables. She adapted the stories for puppets and did all the voices herself, including that of the narrator and all of the characters. She had taken the art of storytelling to a very high level, and her ability to create drama and feeling with her voice (or "voices") was something unforgettable.

After the conference I went over to the sale store these people had set up. There were plenty of puppets for sale and many helpful books. Eleanor Boylan's book, *Holiday Plays for Puppets or People* was there. Boylan has a way of simplifying the dialog and the action for easily adapting the stories for puppet shows. (Since she is a one-woman show, this is necessary.) Her book included not only her adaptions of Aesop but a nice version of the Grimm Brothers' "The Shoemaker and the Elves" for Christmas. This is actually rather a difficult story to match musically. A simple solution might be just to put on some instrumental versions of Christmas carols in the background. I preferred to try a more complicated approach.

I wanted something that was "Christmasy" yet at the same time somber, to reflect the genuine despair and financial trouble of the poor shoemaker and his wife. As the parade of rude, rich, and demanding customers comes in, threatening the over-worked old couple with non-payment if their shoes weren't ready soon, we see the exhaustion and desperation of the man and his wife. They both badly want to sleep, but try to keep working into the night.

The woman finally falls asleep, and the shoemaker hears a knock on the door. The first of the elves arrives, puts the man to sleep, and escorts the rest of the Christmas elves in to finish all the work before morning. Upon the arrival of the elves, the Christmas music should turn from somber to something more upbeat, as we see the fortunes of the shoemaker and his wife going miraculously from poor to very good. How to find a piece of music to do all that?

It took some time, but I eventually found the opening overture from Handel's *Messiah*. The Christmas music has a somber instrumental opening, until suddenly some strong notes from the violins pick up the mood. If you can pace your storytelling to match this transition, you have a perfect pairing. If the somber part is too long, you could start the music a bit of the way into the piece, so that the musical uplift comes at the same time as the arrival of your elves. It just takes a little practice. You could always go back to the Christmas carols if this is too difficult—just stay away from using something too jolly, like "Jingle Bells," at the start, so you don't destroy the mood.

The version of Handel's *Messiah* I use is by Leonard Bernstein and the New York Philharmonic with the Westminster Choir. It is interesting to realize that Handel composed the entire masterpiece between Saturday, August 22 and Monday, September 14, 1741. That's three weeks! It's also nearly 250 years ago. Both of those things give me a feeling of awe as I listen to that music, which is as fresh and lively as if someone had just written it.

These holiday stories are especially challenging musically, but it is an absorbing and interesting challenge.

A Sample Musical Story Hour Program
Theme: Thanksgiving
Ages: Pre-school and early elementary

1. Participation Game: Have children march like a line of turkeys

   Here comes the turkey
   With his funny walk

Gobble, gobble, gobble
Listen to him squawk!
Gobble, gobble, gobble, gobble, gobble

2. Musical Story:

Story:	*Little Bear's Thanksgiving* (Janice)
Music:	"September Song" (an instrumental version—Ruth Welcome's zither arrangement, for example, from her *Sentimental Zither* album)
Musical Mood:	Thoughtful, quiet, warm
Puppet Involvement:	If you have a bear, a girl, a squirrel, a bird, and an owl, and a pillow or cushion for the bed, the puppets can act out on the stage while the storyteller tells the story.

3. Singing:

"Over the River and Through the Woods"

4. Activity:

Draw and photocopy a turkey or a pilgrim for all to color.

References

Cassettes:

Giuliani. Grand Sonata in A Major for Flute and Guitar. *Flute and Guitar—an 18th Century Serenade.* Columbia/Odyssey YT 60218.

Loellet. Sonata in A Minor for Flute and Guitar. *Flute and Guitar—an 18th Century Serenade.* Columbia/Odyssey YT 60218.

Record Albums:

Handel, George Frederick. Overture to *Messiah*. Leonard Bernstein and the New York Philharmonic Orchestra. Columbia Masterworks M2L 242.

"September Song." *Sentimental Zither*. Ruth Welcome. Capital T 2064.

Sousa, John Philip. "El Capitan." *Semper Fidelis: The Marches of John Philip Sousa*. The Goldman Band. Harmony HL 7001.

———. "The Gladiator." *Semper Fidelis: The Marches of John Philip Sousa*. The Goldman Band. Harmony HL 7001.

———. "Stars and Stripes Forever." *Semper Fidelis: The Marches of John Philip Sousa*. The Goldman Band. Harmony HL 7001.

"Tzena, Tzena, Tzena." *The Soul of Israel*. 101 Strings. Alshire S 5044.

Books:

Aleichem, Sholom. *Hanukkah Money*. Greenwillow, 1978.

Boylan, Eleanor. "The Shoemaker and the Elves." Adapted from the Grimm Brothers. In *Holiday Plays for Puppets and People*. New Plays, Inc., 1974.

Carrick, Carol. *A Rabbit for Easter*. Greenwillow, 1979.

Janice, *Little Bear's Thanksgiving*. Lothrop, Lee and Shepard, 1967.

Ross, Laura. "Washington and the First Flight in America." In *Holiday Puppets*. Lothrop, Lee and Shepard, 1974.

13.

Royalty

King Midas and the emperor with his new clothes deserve some stately Handel or baroque trumpet fare

Children's literature is rich in stories involving kings and queens, princes and princesses. It is fun to try to find musical match-ups for such royalty. Let's start by looking at a couple of stories that concern royal garments—"The Emperor's New Clothes" and "Puss in Boots."

Hans Christian Andersen's vain king is told by two swindlers that their clothes are so fine that they become invisible to anyone who is not worthy of his royal position, or who is insufferably dull or stupid. The king and his royal assistants can't admit that they are stupid or unworthy, so they rave about the invisible garments to the weavers. The king strips to let the two clothe him in their fine creations, and off he goes to the royal procession, with royal chamberlains carrying his train, even though they cannot see it.

This part of the story needs no music. The surprise of music with the beginning of the king's naked march is better timed. There are several wonderful choices at this point. Hector Berlioz's version of the Hungarian tune, the "Rakoczy March" (from Berlioz's *Damnation of Faust*) is available on many musical anthologies such as Columbia's *Pomp and Circumstance* album. This particular piece has all the needed ceremonial and marching quality plus an undercurrent of humor as well.

If you would like to try a more formal piece of music and let the humor come from the contrast, there is always the famous piece of "graduation music"—Sir Edward Elgar's *Pomp and Circumstance March no. 1*, the title piece from the same album.

Here the total seriousness of the music both reflects the king's attitude and contrasts with the total ridiculousness of the king's lack of clothing.

Either the Overture Miniature or the following March from Tchaikovsky's *Nutcracker Suite* serve well for this scene. They are both a little lighter than the first two choices, for a less obtrusive approach.

One might even throw subtlety out the window completely and try the French national anthem, "La Marseillaise." Here again is a very funny contrast between the heroic, patriotic anthem and the very unheroic appearance of the marching king, who finally realizes the truth of his predicament when a child says, "But he has nothing on." The king marches on, trying to maintain his dignity in spite of his embarrassing situation!

"Puss in Boots" rather reverses the situation of Andersen's emperor. Poor Carabas goes from nakedness to royal clothing with the help of the talking cat he inherits from his father. "You're lucky you got me," the cat informs Carabas. Puss soon begins to make good on his claim. He goes directly to a brier patch, where he captures a rabbit to take to the king, as a present from the Count of Carabas. Two months worth of gifts to the king, and "the Count" is well known by the royalty. The cat, who brings all the gifts, is decked out in the poor man's hat and boots all the while.

Carabas has few clothes left and he loses them all as Puss tricks him into removing them. The king comes by in his coach, with his beautiful princess daughter, and Puss yells, "Help! Help for the Count of Carabas," further explaining that some villain has stolen the count's clothes while the victim was swimming. The king sends his helper to fetch some of the finest of the royal wardrobe from the castle.

Puss convinces the king that his friend is indeed rich, successful, and kind—and an excellent prospect for the princess. The cat has to eat a ten-foot-tall ogre to do it, but he does manage to convince the king that Carabas owns a castle and has a large kingdom of happy subjects. Sure enough, Carabas winds up as royalty himself, with the lovely princess as his wife.

At the introduction of Puss into the story, it's nice to bring in some theme music for him, like "The Waltzing Cat" by Leroy

Anderson. There is a cassette tape available called *Classical Cats* which offers purely cat themes—like Copland's "The Cat and the Mouse" which could be used when Puss eats the ogre after tricking him into changing into a mouse. On Classical Cats there is also Chopin's Waltz in F (op. 34, no. 3) which makes good theme music for Puss.

As Carabas's fortunes change and it becomes clear that he is destined for a life in the palace with the princess, so too the music changes and becomes equally regal. Mouret's Rondeau (found in the cassette of baroque music called *The Rage of 1710*, and many other anthologies) gives a nice touch to the ending. The trumpet piece may be familiar as the theme from television's "Masterpiece Theater."

Our friend Carabas did not seem destined for major problems like his royal counterpart, King Midas, in a humorous picture book version, *King Midas and the Golden Touch*, by Al Perkins. In this version, the greedy king finds that his touch is turning all he holds dear into cold metal—the royal grape juice, the royal sausages, the blue bird, the frogs, the red roses, and finally his daughter! When the little man with the magical powers breaks the spell, King Midas is ecstatic and un-gilds everything and everybody. "If you love something more than gold, wish for it, King Midas," the little man says, and so the king realizes what is really important to him.

For a musical background to this story you want something regal, but not overbearing, suggesting the loftiness of the king's position and the extent of his treasures, but with a light and upbeat touch. I like the first and third movements (both allegros) of Franz Joseph Haydn's Concerto in E-flat Major for Trumpet and Orchestra, which is widely available on such collections as the *Virtuoso Trumpet, Vol. II*.

Another musical challenge presents itself with a story like Hans Christian Andersen's "The Princess and the Pea." The prince wants to find himself a real princess, but something is always wrong. When a rain-soaked, stringy-haired lady shows up at his doorstep in a storm, claiming to be a real princess, the rainwater gushing through her shoes does not seem to befit the authentic royal quality he has in mind. The old queen places a pea under twenty mattresses and twenty eiderdown beds to test the lady's sensitivity (and thereby her claims) while she sleeps.

Sure enough, our heroine thrashes all night and arises black and blue, proving to the queen that she is indeed a real princess. The rest, as they say, is history.

There is opportunity for a musical change of pace here, because we are dealing with a princess struggling not only with the rain but also with an old queen and a terrible night's sleep. A piece of music that suggests royalty and delicate beauty in a quiet, dignified way, is Johann Sabastian Bach's melodious Air on a G String, which is widely available. It lends itself to a storytelling version in quiet, intimate tones of voice.

Dr. Seuss (with whom we shall spend a chapter later on) has an entry in the royalty stories, *The King's Stilts*. Although King Birtrim never wears his stilts during working hours, he surely loves to race around the palace on them after the official day is done. Old Lord Droon thinks this is too undignified, and so he steals the stilts. Eric the page boy finally rescues the stilts and pulls King Birtrim out of deep despair.

For dramatic effect you can save the music here until the triumphant return of the stilts. The king, "sturdy, straight and strong again, and every inch a king," can be accompanied by a triumphant trumpet, something to let the king strut around to, feeling like a real king again. I use Jeremiah Clarke's "Trumpet Voluntary," which is readily available in many collections of baroque music.

Orchestrating vain kings, a rags-to-riches count, a talking cat, a ruler with magical powers, an old queen, a princess in trouble, and a choosy prince are all challenging experiences. There are many more lesser known royal personages; I have only touched on a few, trying to offer some representative selections which can be used with a wide array of characters interchangeably. The stately music unquestionably adds another enjoyable dimension to the telling of such tales.

Sample Musical Story Hour Program
Theme: Royalty
Ages: 6–10

1. Musical Story:

Story: "The Emperor's New Clothes"

Music: Pomp and Circumstance March no. 1 (Elgar)

Musical   Stately march
Mood:

2. Musical Story:

Story: "Puss in Boots"

Music: "The Waltzing Cat" (Leroy Anderson) and
            Mouret's Rondeau at the end (theme from tele-
            vision's "Masterpiece Theatre")

Musical   Suggestive of a cat, and (at the end) suggestive
Moods: of newfound wealth, good fortune, and position

Puppets: A cat, a man, a princess, and a king

3. Musical Story:

Story: "The Princess and the Pea"

Music: Bach's Air on a G String

Musical   Delicate, quiet
Moods:

Puppets: You could use one princess, one prince, a
            queen, a pea, and anything resembling mat-
            tresses (a pile of sponges will do) for this one.

References

Cassettes:

Bach, Johann Sebastian. Air on a G String. *The Rage of 1710*. Vox/
    Turnabout CT 4713.

Chopin, Frederic. Waltz in F, opus 34, no. 3. *Classical Cats*.
    London PS5 922.

Clarke, Jeremiah. "Trumpet Voluntary." *The Rage of 1710*. Vox/
    Turnabout CT 4713.

Copland, Aaron. "The Cat and the Mouse." *Classical Cats.* London PS5 922.

Haydn, Franz Joseph. Concerto in E-flat Major for Trumpet and Orchestra. *The Virtuoso Trumpet. Vol. II. Music for One, Two and Six Trumpets.* The Bach Guild Historical Anthology of Music CHM 63.

Mouret, Rondeau. *The Rage of 1710.* Vox/Turnabout CT 4713.

Record Albums:

Anderson, Leroy. "The Waltzing Cat." *Fiddle Faddle.* Arthur Fiedler and the Boston Pops. RCA Victor LM/LSC-2638.

Berlioz, Hector. "The Rakoczy March." *Pomp and Circumstance.* Capitol SP 8620.

Elgar, Edward. "Pomp and Circumstance March" no. 1. *Pomp and Circumstance.* Capitol SP 8620.

"La Marseillaise." *Pomp and Circumstance.* Capitol SP 8620.

Tchaikovsky, Peter. "Overture Miniature." *The Nutcracker Suite.* Arturo Toscanini and the NBC Symphony Orchestra. RCA Victor LM-1986.

————. March. *The Nutcracker Suite.* Arturo Toscanini and the NBC Symphony Orchestra. RCA Victor LM-1986.

Books:

Andersen, Hans Christian. "The Emperor's New Clothes." *Andersen's Fairy Tales.* Grosset and Dunlap, 1945.

————. "The Princess and the Pea." *The Andrew Lang Fairy Tale Treasury.* Avenel, 1979.

Dr. Seuss. *The King's Stilts.* Random House, 1939, 1967.

Latham, Jean Lee, reteller. *Puss in Boots.* Bobbs-Merrill, 1961.

Perkins, Al, reteller. *King Midas and the Golden Touch.* Random House Beginner Books, 1969.

14.

Off the Wall Stories and Music

The Stupids meet Spike Jones
(and other inspired combinations)

Some stories would have to be labeled "off the wall" in modern slang, or "novelty stories," in more conventional language. It can be a real challenge to find music that works with them.

Two favorite stories for telling are Harry Allard's *The Stupids Die* and *The Stupids Have a Ball*. In the first, we meet the Stupids eating breakfast in a shower, with Stanley complaining that his eggs are runny! Later, after son Buster mows the carpet, the Stupids relax in front of the television set when suddenly the lights go out in the house. "We must be dead," Stanley reasons. The dog ("Kitty") and the cat ("Xylophone") go to the basement to replace the fuse. When the lights go back on, Stanley figures they are all in heaven. Grandfather Stupid bursts through the front door on his motorcycle and Stanley welcomes him to heaven. "This is Cleveland." Realizing the truth, the Stupids put on their sneakers and go to bed.

One of the few advantages to being over forty is being able to remember music from many years ago that people in their twenties and thirties never even heard of. If you happen to be writing a book on the subject, this can be of particular value! The music I chose to go along with the Stupids' trip to heaven is Spike Jones's old classic novelty version of "Holiday for Strings." In the hands of Spike Jones, the title is a misnomer, for he uses everything but strings—bicycle horns, kazoos, slide whistles, washboards, tubas. Maybe there are even some strings hidden in there, but they're not prominent.

There is probably no orchestra today (or in recent memory)

comparable to the Spike Jones ensembles. If you've never heard their music, it's rather difficult to describe, other than to say it is novelty music, mixing normal instruments with unusual ones, and adding hiccups, burps, raspberries, screams, lisps, war chants, and impersonations. Everest/Europa has a current cassette tape out called *Spike Jones's Greatest Hits*. This music may not be up there with the Mozart concertos but it suits the Stupids perfectly.

In the second Allard book, *The Stupids Have a Ball*, the lovable parents decide to throw a special party on the glorious occasion of their children's having flunked all their school subjects. All the relatives come, including Grandfather Stupid and Cousin Dottie. Grandfather dances with her and says, "You sure can polka, Dot."

I have often thought in jest that someone might even use Lawrence Welk with a story. Here he comes! *Polkas*, a Welk album featuring Myron Floren on the accordion, is a good choice here. "The Hoop Dee Doo Polka" or "Just Because" both add a jolly tempo to the nonsensical dancing party, and give a perfect flavor to the telling of the tale.

Myron Floren, incidentally, is not widely known for his other contributions to music aside from appearing with the Welk orchestra, but he *has* composed over sixty original musical works and published twenty books on the accordion!

As the Stupids' ball continues, the cat and dog make punch, freely adding tuna fish, catsup, and pepper to the bowl. "I wonder what the secret ingredients are," Mrs. Stupid gushes with admiration.

Spike Jones's "Cocktails for Two" fits well here also. There is some vocal in the piece which is usually to be avoided so as not to conflict with the storytelling. However, it gets so lost among the special effects that, in this case, the presence of words doesn't matter. No one will notice! Like the Stupids, everyone will have a wonderful time.

There are some "off the wall" picture books which concern the favorite hobby of many—jogging, and treat it humourously. *The Adventures of Albert the Running Bear* is a good example. Barbara Isenberg's little circus bear is sent to the zoo when the circus goes out of business. He performs for the zoo spectators also, juggling and dancing. People throw him treats like marsh-mallows and gumdrops. Soon the zoo doctor diagnoses Albert as too fat and bans the feeding of treats by the public. With the aid of a giraffe, Albert escapes from his cage and searches the city for food. Holing up in a well stocked garbage can, Albert falls blissfully asleep until he is tossed into a garbage truck. He finds a red jogging outfit in the truck, which he promptly puts on. As he leaps out of the vehicle, he finds himself in the middle of a group of runners in a race. Eventually, another runner grabs him and says, "Let's go!" Albert goes, and wins the marathon.

Back at the zoo, they build a quarter-mile track for Albert to show off his running skill every day for zoo visitors. People come from miles away each day to see him.

It takes a little patience to find the musical passages suitable for this story. Once you have them, you could simplify things by tape recording them so that you don't have to search all over the records when you are telling the stories. The peppy main themes from Liszt's Hungarian Rhapsody no. 2 and Georges Enesco's Roumanian Rhapsody no. 1 are great surprises to play, just at the point where Albert lands in the middle of the race. The unbridled vigor of both pieces make them great match-ups for a marathon race.

Jack Kent's *Silly Goose* gives us still another jogger or two. The goose and fox are both jogging through the woods. The goose tries to warn the fox that an *elm* tree is falling toward him. Disdainful of the advice from the silly goose because the smart fox knows it is an *oak* tree, he runs directly under it. The goose digs the fox out.

The goose also warns the fox about a lurking crocodile, but the fox again disdains the warning because he knows it's an alligator, even as it swallows him. Another rescue is needed. Still another mix-up involves an eagle and a buzzard. By the end of the book, we know which jogger is silly and which is wise.

With this fast-moving story, you can use a little classical piece by Ries called "Perpetual Motion." It is just what the title implies—a lot of violins in constant staccato melodies. It makes a nice background mood for our "off the wall" joggers.

Another runner for which "Perpetual Motion" works well is

Joey the kangaroo baby in Jack Kent's book *Joey Runs Away*. Joey's mother asks the boy to clean up his room (her pouch), so he runs away from home. He tries to find a new place to live and winds up in a pelican's pouch. A wild flight follows, for which that music is appropriate. It's also fitting that when Joey makes it back home, he cleans up his room.

An "off the wall" story that human mothers will identify with is the story of poor old Mrs. Large, the elephant mother of three—Lester, Laura, and the baby. Jill Murphy's charming book, *Five Minutes' Peace*, recounts the futile efforts of Mrs. Large to find that much rest from her horde of wild elephants. They even invade her bubble bath, blasting the silence and serenity with their musical instruments, toys, books, and chatter. Three minutes and forty-five seconds is about all Mrs. Large can put together.

Harking back to an earlier musical piece, Camille Saint-Saens's *Carnival of the Animals* has a section called "The Elephant." The humorously slow and ponderous rhythms of this music seem to reflect the exhaustion and resignation in the daily life of poor Mrs. Large.

All of Peggy Parish's Amelia Bedelia books could be considered "off the wall." Since Ms. Parish used to be a school teacher in Oklahoma, Kentucky, and New York, she seems to have a special feeling for *Teach Us, Amelia Bedelia*.

For these books it's good to have something light and cheerful going in the background. So many sections of Franz Joseph Haydn's symphonies have this quality—understated and unobtrusive, yet full of the irrepressible good cheer of Amelia Bedelia. I like the second and third movements of Symphony no. 94 ("Surprise") for these stories.

In her role as a substitute teacher, Amelia plants bulbs (light bulbs), calls the roll ("Roll! Hey, roll," she calls to the roll she borrowed from Peter's lunch box), and has the children paint pictures—as her instructions say. She has them paint on all the pictures that are hanging on the wall. The "Surprise" symphony may be especially appropriate, as the real teacher is surely in for a surprise when she comes and sees the pictures.

I hope you have gotten some ideas from this rhapsodical romp through some favorite unusual stories. They are definitely fun to tell, and fun for the children to hear. A little background music will make them even more delightful for all concerned.

A Sample Musical Story Hour Program
Theme: Off the Wall Stories and Games
Ages: 6–10

1. Participation Game: My Name's Joe

(Ask the children to stand up, repeat each line after you, and do everything you do.)

Hi, my name's Joe.
I've got a wife and three kids.
I work in a button factory.
One day the boss came in,
And he said, "Joe, are you busy?"
And I said, "No."
So he said, "Do it like this."
(Move right hand in circles and don't stop.)

Hi, my name's Joe.
I've got a wife and three kids.
I work in a button factory.
One day the boss came in,
And he said, "Joe, are you busy?"
And I said, "No."
So he said, "Do it like this."
(Move left hand in circles and don't stop.
Now both hands are going in circles.)

Hi, my name's Joe.
I've got a wife and three kids.
I work in a button factory.
One day the boss came in,
And he said, "Joe, are you busy?"
And I said, "No."

So he said, "Do it like this."
(Move right foot in circles, along with hands.)

Hi, my name's Joe.
I've got a wife and three kids.
I work in a button factory.
One day the boss came in,
And he said, "Joe, are you busy?"
And I said, "No."
So he said, "Do it like this."
(Alternate one foot then the other, in circles, along with hands.)

Hi, my name's Joe.
I've got a wife and three kids.
I work in a button factory.
One day the boss came in,
And he said, "Joe, are you busy?"
And I said, "YES!"
That's how Joe finally got *smart*!

2. Musical Story:

Story: *The Stupids Die* (Allard)

Music: "Holiday for Strings" (Spike Jones)

Musical   Full of humor and odd sounds, lively
Mood:

3. Musical Story:

Story: *The Stupids Have a Ball* (Allard)

Music: "Just Because" (Myron Floren)

Musical   Party time (any lively polka music would do)
Mood:

4. Filmstrip:

I Know an Old Lady Who Swallowed a Fly (Weston Woods)

5. Musical Story:

Story: *Albert the Running Bear* (Isenberg)

Music: Melody from Hungarian Rhapsody no. 2 (Liszt)

Musical   Fast, upbeat, loaded with energy, exciting, me-
Mood: lodious

Puppets: You could use a bear, a giraffe, and a man (jogger) for this one. These few characters are behind you on the stage as you tell the story out
front with the book.

References

Cassettes:

"Cocktails for Two." *Spike Jones's Greatest Hits*. Everest/Europa 818.

Haydn, Franz Joseph. Symphony no. 94 (*Surprise* Symphony). CBS MP-39025.

"Holiday for Strings." *Spike Jones's Greatest Hits*. Everest/Europa 818.

Saint-Saens, Camille. "The Elephant." *Carnival of the Animals*. Seraphim 4XG-60214.

Record Albums:

Enesco, Georges. Roumanian Rhapsody no. 2. *Rhapsodies*. Columbia ML 5299.

"Hoop Dee Doo Polka." *Polkas with Lawrence Welk*. Myron Floren, accordionist. Dot DLP 25302.

"Just Because." *Polkas with Lawrence Welk*. Myron Floren, accordionist. Dot DLP 25302.

Liszt, Franz. Hungarian Rhapsody no. 2. *Rhapsodies*. Columbia ML 5299.

Ries. "Perpetual Motion." *Popular Classics, Volume 2.* Morton Gould and his Orchestra. RCA VICS-1381.

Books:

Allard, Harry. *The Stupids Die.* Houghton Mifflin, 1981.

————. *The Stupids Have a Ball.* Houghton Mifflin, 1978.

Isenberg, Barbara. *The Adventures of Albert the Running Bear.* Clarion, 1982.

Kent, Jack. *Silly Goose.* Prentice-Hall, 1983.

Murphy, Jill. *Five Minutes' Peace.* G. P. Putnam's Sons, 1986.

Parish, Peggy. *Teach Us, Amelia Bedelia.* Greenwillow, 1977.

15.

Dance

From *Swan Lake* to the "Waltz of the
Flowers" to polka music; such rhythms
can set a tone and pace for dance stories

There's no way to bring classical ballet music into the story
we're going to start with, so we'll have to go to the big dance
bands of the swing era. Benny Goodman and Glenn Miller are
needed for this story, but we'll bring in some classical ballet
later in the chapter.

Isadora by Jody Silver is a book whose title suggests the fine
and famous dancer, Isadora Duncan, but it is not. Our heroine
here is a donkey—but what a gal! All the illustrations in this
wonderful book are in black and white, except for the bright red
of the feather boa which Isadora sees in a store and wants to
buy to wear around her neck. To her, it is like a mink stole, an
infinitely desired and special scarf, and she can not resist buying
it. She is a bit too shy at first to wear it in public, but when she
tries it in front of her mirror at home she shouts, "Ta Daaa!" As
she does her housework and sees how plain she looks without
it, she frets. Grabbing her red boa, Isadora begins to dance with
glee. "Isadora, you're adorable," she tells herself! She dances
so happily that the neighbor underneath her apartment com-
plains.

It is at this point that Benny Goodman or Glenn Miller can
add a nice touch to the telling. The album, *The Famous Goodman
1938 Jazz Concert in Carnegie Hall* is a recording of such a historic
concert in the annals of American music that it should always
be fairly easy to obtain. Goodman's band members read like a
who's who of American popular music. Gene Krupa on the
drums turned the stately Carnegie Hall into a frenzied mass of

shrieking devotees of swing. Harry James and Ziggy Elman provided a one-two punch in the trumpet section. The King of Swing featured Lionel Hampton on the vibraphone and Teddy Wilson on the piano. Count Basie sat in for this concert.

Any number of Goodman classics would be nice, danceable background for the delightful, spontaneous, joyful jigs of our girl Isadora—"One O'Clock Jump," "When My Baby Smiles at Me," "I Got Rhythm," or "Stompin' at the Savoy."

Benny Goodman, incidentally, was just as much at home playing Mozart's Clarinet Concerto as "One O'Clock Jump." He was indeed a gifted musician, and he knew it too. When someone asked him "How long an intermission do you want?" Goodman is quoted as replying, "I dunno, how much does Toscanini have?"

Glenn Miller is another excellent choice for Isadora. "In the Mood," "Tuxedo Junction," and "Little Brown Jug" are a few of his classics from 1939 and 1940 that could well set her feet tapping.

A couple of picture books that concern formal ballet classes might be more likely candidates for classical ballet music. Rachel Isadora's *My Ballet Class* is a serious look at a children's ballet lesson. Wouldn't you know, by the way, that someone with the last name of Isadora would write a book on ballet! Anyway, here we have a little white girl and her black girl friend learning how to do a plié, an arabesque, a developpé à la seconde, from Mr. Lucien the dance instructor. They also practice the five basic positions, and (aside from an occasional giggle) they also learn that there will be no talking during class.

One girl's favorite music to dance to, she tells us, is *Swan Lake*. This, of course, gives us a natural choice for music to use with this particular story. The story itself may be rather limited for a general story hour, unless you know of a special interest in ballet in the group, or have a special performer for the program. Also, Tchaikovsky's *Swan Lake* is a long piece, and it's necessary to pick a section.

Probably the showcase number from the piece is the "Waltz of the Swans" and this would be the best choice. It has all the drama and pageantry a dancer could ask for. The "Valse-

Bluette" is a bit slower and toned down, if you prefer that approach.

A more generally usable picture book on dance for storytelling is Helen Oxenbury's *The Dancing Class*. In this, listeners can more easily identify with the heroine than with the serious dancer of Rachel Isadora's book. Here the little girl is trying it out. She doesn't tie her shoelaces very well and eventually they become loose, so the would-be prima ballerina falls flat on her face, knocking an entire group of girls gracefully to the floor with her. All is forgiven, though, and the lesson goes on.

The fun of a book like this can be using some grand and glorious ballet music in the background to create a contrast with the clutzy budding ballerina. Chopin's ballet music, *Les Sylphides*, is a nice contrast. It is a ballet without a story. The dancing sylphs enter a moonlit glade and dance to the music. This fairy-like, exquisitely graceful music makes a nice foil for a girl with loose shoelaces.

Margaret Rey's *Curious George at the Ballet* is another story that can be enhanced with a grand and serious musical background as contrast. Our legendary monkey's curiosity always gets him into trouble, and in this case puts George in the middle of a ballet production in front of an audience. George is no Baryshnikov or Nureyev, but some majestic Tchaikovsky, such as "Sleeping Beauty Waltz," adds a neat touch to his predicament.

Another terrific foil for Curious George is the melodious and graceful "Waltz of the Flowers" from the *Nutcracker Suite*. Augusta Baker mentioned a kindergarten teacher using this piece with some slides of flowers in bloom, in her classic book, *Storytelling: Art and Technique*. There are many stories of the dance and others about flowers with which you could use this piece. *The Story of Ferdinand*, the bull who loved to sniff flowers, by Munro Leaf, comes to mind. It can serve as a lovely backdrop to serious stories or as a humorous contrast to stories like *Curious George at the Ballet*.

Another type of dance story is represented by Ruth Bornstein's *The Dancing Man*. This is a seriously told, fanciful story of a poor orphan boy, Joseph, from a village on the Baltic Sea. He notices that the trees dance, fire dances, the clouds and the sun dance—and he would like to dance too. An old man appears, dancing on the waves, and comes to shore to give Joseph a gift of silver dancing shoes. When the boy is grown enough to fit the shoes, he does indeed dance away from the poverty of his village, going from town to town, like the old dancing man had done, making a living by bringing the joy of his dancing to all he meets. As Joseph goes from town to town he grows older and older. By the time he reaches the southernmost sea, he too has become an old man. Joseph spots a young boy, takes off the silver shoes to give away, and introduces himself—"I'm the Dancing Man."

If you're going to try ballet music with this, you have to be careful to find something which is not too feminine for the character. There are parts of *Coppelia* by Delibes which you can use, but you have to hunt and choose them. An easier choice to locate is the "Arabian Dance" from Tchaikovsky's *Nutcracker Suite*.

Let's take one more type of dance book before leaving this subject. George Shannon's *Dance Away* is about a rabbit who loves to dance. Dancing with his rabbit friends is great fun, until one day they stop dancing. They are trapped by a fox. The desperate rabbit tries to buy time, asking the fox if he'll allow one more dance with his friends.

All the rabbits, and finally the fox, join in the catchy celebration of the moment. Rabbit calls out the steps and all the others follow along. They come to the river and Rabbit yells for the fox to jump, with all the rabbits holding on to him. The fox jumps and, while he is in mid-air heading down, the rabbits leap off him to the safety of the far bank.

I like a peppy, short waltz for this story, like the "Gold and Silver Waltz" by Lehar. It's a six-minute piece of sprightly fluff (much like the rabbits) which adds a nice pace to the story.

Humphrey, the Dancing Pig by Arthur Getz offers a rare opportunity to do a dance spectacular with a lot of humor and a variety of musical accompaniments. It helps if you have a pig puppet bedecked in various costumes to add something visual in motion.

Humphrey is such a fat pig that he wants to become slim like the cat, so he takes up dancing. Every day he tries a different dance—a cossack dance, an Indian dance, a rock 'n' roll dance, ballet, an acrobatic dance, a Hawaiian hula, and a whirling dervish routine. The new, skinny Humphrey emerges.

The farmer, annoyed that Humphrey wants to be like the cat, makes him chase mice and rats. Because of his indignation at this, Humphrey discards his diet, eats like a pig again, regains his full figure, and returns the mice-chasing job to the cat.

The individual dance segments of this story lend themselves to a potentially hilarious combination of music and story and puppetry.

The Russian cossack dance could be represented by the "Russian Dance" ("Trepak") from Tchaikovsky's *Nutcracker Suite*. The pig puppet can do his dance for about thirty seconds until someone slowly turns down the sound and the storyteller intones, ". . . and the next day Humphrey did an *Indian* dance."

Any American Indian music will do. Perhaps you can add a headdress and feathers to your pig puppet and have him dance to the Indian rhythms of the third movement (Scherzo) of Dvořák's *New World* Symphony.

You can have some fun when Humphrey takes up rock 'n' roll. A few bars of Little Richard's version of "Good Golly, Miss Molly" would wake up an audience in a hurry! Your choice is wide open here. "Hound Dog"? "Twist and Shout"?

Whatever you pick, the ensuing ballet segment should be a slow, elegant contrast, like the "Waltz of the Flowers," from the *Nutcracker Suite* again.

Acrobatic music follows, and this could be circus calliope music like "The Man on the Flying Trapeze."

When Humphrey takes to trying the hula, you could add a grass skirt and a lei to your pig puppet and put on some Hawaiian music like "Little Grass Shack" from the 101 Strings's *Hawaiian Paradise* album.

The whirling dervish dance Humphrey does could be matched by any type of swirling fast music—a Paganini caprice or violin concerto, "Perpetual Motion" by Ries, some lively jazz or dixieland, or banjo music, like the lively "Flop-Eared Mule" from *Feuding Banjos*.

Humphrey the Dancing Pig is a special kind of story since it gives us a chance to really try some creative things with it.

This is also a theme that can be used for more than just

entertainment. Recently a fourth-grade teacher called to ask if we could do a puppet show and book display on "fears," for a class visit.

I picked Nancy Carlson's book *Harriet's Recital*, which deals with stage fright. It makes a great puppet show as well. Harriet the dog loves her ballet class, except for the yearly recital. Her knees shake and she's terrified that her outfit will rip. Finally, she faces up to her fear and goes out on the stage, and does very well.

At the moment she goes out on the stage, I switch from storyteller to full-blown puppeteer, putting on the "Dance of the Sugar Plum Fairies" from Tchaikovsky's *Nutcracker Suite*. Out come the "classmates" behind the Harriet (dog) puppet—a dancing hippo and eight long-legged "gangly" puppets, (donated by a local department store) in a cute, funny, and wordless ballet dance.

It brings some humor to a serious discussion of children's fears, and an introduction to books about fears and problems, following the show.

A Sample Musical Story Hour Program
Theme: Dance
Ages: 3–8

1. Activity: "The Hokey Pokey"

Since the theme of this program is dance, we can use the old standard, "The Hokey Pokey." There are numerous recordings available in case you absolutely can't sing:

(Children form a circle)

You put your right foot in
You put your right foot out
You put your right foot in
And shake it all about

You do the Hokey Pokey and you
   turn yourself around
That's what it's all about

(For the verses that follow, substitute for "right foot": left foot, right hand, left hand, head and whole self.)

2. Musical Story:

Story: *Isadora* (Jody Silver)

Music: "One O'Clock Jump" (Benny Goodman)

Musical   Jazzy, fun lively
Mood:

3. Musical Story:

Story: *The Dancing Class* (Helen Oxenbury)

Music: *Les Sylphides* (Chopin)

Musical   Majestic and grand, in contrast to the clutzy
Mood: dancer.

Puppets: A clutzy looking girl ballerina and some less clutzy ballerinas could be good. You may have to make the tutus since commercial puppets like this are tough to find.

4. Musical Story:

Story: *Curious George at the Ballet* (Rey)

Music: "Waltz of the Flowers" (Tchaikovsky)

Musical   Melodious and lovely, in contrast to the trouble-
Mood: some monkey.

Puppets: A monkey and some dancers. These are behind you on the stage, as you tell the story with the book out front.

5. Activity:

Coloring. A ballet dancer in costume.

References

Cassettes:

Chopin, Frederic. *Les Sylphides*. *Les Sylphides, Sylvia, Coppelia, Ballet Suites*. CBS Odyssey YT 39506.

Delibes. *Coppelia*. *Les Sylphides, Sylvia, Coppelia, Ballet Suites*. CBS Odyssey YT 39506.

"In the Mood." *Glenn Miller and His Orchestra*. SAAR MC 3865.

"Little Brown Jug." *Glenn Miller and His Orchestra*. SAAR MC 3865.

"The Man on the Flying Trapeze." *Circus Calyope*. Gay 90s Village 5174–67.

Record Albums:

Dvořàk, Antonin. Scherzo. *The New World Symphony*. Westminster XWN-18295.

"Flop Eared Mule." *Feuding Banjos*. Olympic 7105.

"I Got Rhythm." *Benny Goodman—The Famous 1938 Carnegie Hall Jazz Concert*. Volume 2. Columbia CL 815.

"Little Grass Shack." *101 Strings in a Hawaiian Paradise*. Somerset SF-12800.

"One O'Clock Jump." *Benny Goodman—The Famous 1938 Carnegie Hall Jazz Concert*. Volume 1. Columbia CL 814.

"Stompin at the Savoy." *Benny Goodman—The Famous 1938 Carnegie Hall Jazz Concert*. Volume 3. Columbia CL 816.

Tchaikovsky, Peter. "Arabian Dance." *Nutcracker Suite*. Arturo Toscanini and the NBC Symphony Orchestra. RCA Victor LM-1986.

———. "Dance of the Sugar Plum Fairies." *Nutcracker Suite*. Arturo Toscanini and the NBC Symphony Orchestra. RCA Victor LM-1986.

———. "Russian Dance." *Nutcracker Suite*. Arturo Toscanini and the NBC Symphony Orchestra. RCA Victor LM-1986.

————. "Sleeping Beauty." *The Wonderful Waltzes of Tchaikovsky.* Morton Gould and the Chicago Symphony Orchestra. RCA Victor LSC-2890.

————. "Valse-Bluette." *The Wonderful Waltzes of Tchaikovsky.* Morton Gould and the Chicago Symphony Orchestra. RCA Victor LSC-2890.

————. "The Waltz of the Flowers." *Nutcracker Suite.* Arturo Toscanini and the NBC Symphony Orchestra. RCA Victor LM-1986.

————. "Waltz of the Swans." *The Wonderful Waltzes of Tchaikovsky.* Morton Gould and the Chicago Symphony Orchestra. RCA Victor LSC-2890.

"When My Baby Smiles at Me." *Benny Goodman—The Famous 1938 Carnegie Hall Jazz Concert.* Volume 1. Columbia CL 814.

Books:

Baker, Augusta. *Storytelling. Art and Technique.* Bowker, 1987.

Bornstein, Ruth. *The Dancing Man.* Seabury Press, 1978.

Carlson, Nancy. *Harriet's Recital.* Carolrhoda, 1982.

Getz, Arthur. *Humphrey the Dancing Pig.* Dial, 1980.

Isadora, Rachel. *My Ballet Class.* Greenwillow, 1980.

Leaf, Munro. *The Story of Ferdinand.* Viking, 1936.

Oxenbury, Helen. *The Dancing Class.* Walker Books, Ltd., 1983.

Rey, Margaret. *Curious George at the Ballet.* Houghton Mifflin, 1986.

Shannon, George. *Dance Away.* Greenwillow, 1982.

Silver, Jody. *Isadora.* Doubleday, 1981.

16.

Caldecott Award Winners

Orchestrating the best is a special challenge

The Caldecott Medal winners—what a wonderland of material to match with music! The winners of the award for the best illustrations offer such a rich array of delight, it's hard to know where to start.

Paul Goble's 1978 winner, *The Girl Who Loved Wild Horses,* makes an interesting pairing with the Indian themes of Dvořák's third movement of his *New World* Symphony, so we'll start there.

Goble's Indian heroine is always around the wild horses. One day a thunderstorm drives her and the horses from their home, away to the moonlit cliffs where a mighty stallion welcomes the girl to live with them. Eventually according to the legend, she becomes one of them.

Antonin Dvořák became director of the National Conservatory of Music in New York in 1892. Here Professor Dvořák began searching out Indian and Negro folk melodies to incorporate into his symphonic efforts. He was even known for stopping to listen to itinerant street singers, collecting melodies and leaving a little money with them, as well. Dvořák was always trying to catch some new phrase of musical expression.

"The Song of Hiawatha," the poem about Indians by Henry Wadsworth Longfellow, is said to have influenced Dvořák when he wrote the famous *New World* Symphony (Symphony no. 5 in E minor). The mood of the third movement clearly reflects American Indian influence, and it goes well with the Indian girl's story in Paul Goble's beautiful book.

The same music could also be used with the other American Indian Caldecott-winning story, Gerald McDermott's *Arrow to the Sun, a Pueblo Indian Tale.* Here again is a legendary story, involving an Indian boy who seeks his father, the Lord of the Sun. In both stories the Indian rhythms Dvořák gathered for the music add a nice background for the storyteller.

Let's move on from American Indian music to some African background for a story like Marcia Brown's *Shadow*. Brown is to date, the only three-time Caldecott Medal winner, for *Cinderella*, *Once a Mouse*, and *Shadow*. Many of her other books have been Caldecott Honor books, including *Stone Soup*, *Dick Whittington and His Cat*, *Puss in Boots*, and *The Steadfast Tin Soldier*.

Shadow is one of the most memorable of her books, and indeed, of all the Caldecott winners. Brown's use of silhouettes is especially creative and effective in evoking the feeling of Africa. The village storytellers and shamans spun tales, and this particular look at the eerie Shadow was captured by the French poet, Blaise Cendrars, and translated by Brown.

Although it is usually best to avoid music with words for our purpose, here is a case in which to make an exception. It was Harry Belafonte who introduced many Americans to Miriam Makeba's African music, appearing with her in concerts. There are quite a few of her recordings in which she uses an African language rather than English, and you will find that these do not interfere with the words of the storyteller.

The recording, *The World of Miriam Makeba*, has a song called "Into Yam" which makes a terrific background for a story like *Shadow*. Makeba is a South African Xosa tribeswoman, so her sound is genuine and authentic.

Miriam Makeba's music also can be used with Gail E. Haley's Caldecott winner about Ananse, the Spider Man, *A Story, A Story*. Once there were no stories, she tells us, and Ananse wanted to buy them from the Sky God. The price is that Ananse capture Osebo the leopard, Mmbora the hornet, and Mmoatia the fairy. When Ananse accomplishes all these, he gains the stories and brings them to the people of the earth. The African chant "Dubula" from the same Makeba album fits very well with this particular story.

Take a look now at one of the treasures of the Caldecott collection, a nice story to use for an Easter program, *The Egg Tree* by Katherine Milhous. This 1951 winner has an Easter egg hunt on Grandma's Pennsylvania farm as its focus. Katy and Carl visit their cousins, Appolonia and Luke, Susy and Johnny, and they all compete to find the most eggs. Katy finds a long forgotten stash of eggs that Grandma had blown out, colored and hidden when she herself had been young.

The family proceeds to do something special with the eggs, displaying them on a small tree, with string holding them on, through small holes. Thus begins a tradition of the egg tree. The number of eggs grows each year and the size of the tree grows along with them. People start coming, as a tradition, to see the tree.

There are several sections of Beethoven's Symphony no. 6 (*Pastoral* Symphony) which evoke a feeling with which the story is imbued. The names describing the movements will give you a clue as to the contents, if you've not heard them. The first movement of this 1808 symphony is titled "Cheerful impressions awakened by arrival in the country." This is probably the best section to use, although the third movement, "Merry gathering of country folk" is also appropriate. The more bucolic and light feeling of the first movement is preferable to the more robust dance rhythms of the third, but either fits the mood. Of course, when you're dealing with Beethoven, even at his most bucolic, it's best to keep the volume down fairly low because he tends to build to crescendos every so often.

My own favorite Caldecott book has always been *A Tree is Nice*, Janice Udry's 1957 winner illustrated by Marc Simont. This may be because it's the very first Caldecott book I ever picked up—back in library school at Louisiana State University.

There is an extremely nice, quiet, gentle piece of music to go with this elegantly simple story—Gluck's "Dance of the Blessed Spirits" from his opera, *Orfeo and Eurydice*. The blessed spirits being evoked could just as well be the gently blowing leaves. The piece is a particularly good match for this book, as the musical imagery truly does suggest the natural beauty pictured in the book.

Robert McCloskey's 1942 Caldecott winner, *Make Way for Ducklings*, is another book featuring a good deal of natural beauty—in the parks and lakes of Boston. The setting, however, is a backdrop for the story of the ducklings marching along. Who will ever forget the picture of the kindly policeman stopping the traffic in all directions so that the ducklings can march across a busy road safely, on their way to the park?

Since this march is the focal point of the story, some light marching music makes a good background for it. I like my calliope version of "Colonel Bogey's March" (from the movie *The Bridge on the River Kwai*). This is found on the tape mentioned earlier, *Circus Calyope*.

Of course, the "March King" is still John Philip Sousa, even though he died in 1932. His marches are still as fresh and alive as they were then. A nice selection for our marching ducklings is "The Washington Post March"—a lighter pick than, say, "Stars and Stripes Forever"—and perfectly in step with the ducks.

The 1970 Caldecott winner is especially good for telling: William Steig's *Sylvester and the Magic Pebble.* The pictures are so large, clear, and colorful that they are easily seen from all parts of the room.

The structure of the story makes for an interesting search for appropriate musical background. It starts off happily enough, with Sylvester Duncan the donkey enjoying a normal life with his parents. Things suddenly change when he finds the magic red pebble. Although he has fun turning the rain on and off with it, Sylvester panics when he sees a lion, and wishes he were a rock. Sylvester's wish becomes reality, and so his parents spend most of the book searching in vain for their lost boy. They are very sad, but after the long winter they decide to try to be happy again. They go on a picnic using the rock (Sylvester) as their table. They find the magic pebble and think how much Sylvester would have liked it. They pick up the pebble and place it on the rock. Sylvester, touching his magic pebble, wishes he were his old self again, and so is transformed. The dishes fall to the ground as Sylvester returns to donkeyhood and all is well again.

This seems to call for two separate pieces of music to create the opposite moods of happiness and despair. Two selections by Felix Mendelssohn work well to create these moods. His "Spring Song" is a light, cheerful, and familiar melody which sets the tone for the family togetherness at the beginning. The more plaintive and wistful sounds of Russian violinist David

Oistrakh, playing "On Wings of Song," make an appropriate interlude while Sylvester is lost and his parents are searching for him. As the magic pebble works its wonders once more, and the joyous donkey returns to his family, "Spring Song" again fills the bill for this springtime happy reunion at the picnic. This, of course, requires a helper at the stereo—a person with a good sense of timing. Since our stereo is behind the scenes of the puppet stage, the changing of the records can be done unobtrusively while the story is read out front, with a few puppets to reinforce the visual aspects.

Our room is set up so that we can turn off the lights in the room, except for the fluorescent light in the top of the puppet stage which also lights the book for reading, the teller sitting on a stool in front.

One of the most delightful of the Caldecott Award winners is 1952's purely fun story, *Finders Keepers*, by Lipkind and Mordvinoff. Nap and Winkle, the two dogs who find a bone, spend the greater part of the story arguing over whose it should be. One saw it first, but the other touched it first. No one the silly dogs ask seems to be able to solve their dilemma until a big, black dog solves it by taking it himself. Suddenly united, Nap and Winkle attack the larger dog, "wrassle" away their bone and forever learn the wisdom of sharing.

I'd stay with Mendelssohn again for this one. The Violin Concerto's third and final movement has plenty of pep and playfulness to it, and the violin itself suggests a lot of movement from place to place. It's a nice piece to use all the way through the story.

If, however, you have enough help and you want to get fancy with the background, you could throw in a good "galop" to go with the scene where the two dogs attack the big dog who steals their bone. Liszt's "Grand Galop Chromatique" makes good "dog-wrasslin' " background, as does Kabalevsky's "Galop" from *The Comedians*. It may be better to keep things simple, but there are plenty of options!

Try as I might, I could not come up with a piece of classical Japanese music to use with Arlene Mosel's *The Funny Little Woman*. I can hear the title character laughing at me, "Tee-he-

he-he," as she sees me straining my brain and my music collection to think of something I might have heard.

The little woman from old Japan drops her dumpling down a hole and goes down after it. The wicked one captures her to cook for him. After much time goes by, she escapes, bringing home a magic paddle which helps her make so many rice dumplings to sell that she becomes the richest woman in all Japan. Blair Lent's drawings make all this quite believable!

I did manage to find a Japanese tune, "Sukiyaka," (which was a popular hit in the U.S. in the sixties) on an album called *Walt Disney Presents It's a Small World—18 Favorite Folk Songs*. It makes a nice background for many an Oriental story, and the Japanese lyrics don't conflict with anyone's ability to understand your storytelling in English.

The Caldecott Winners—and the Honor Books—offer such a rich variety of material, it is really challenging to find good musical background for telling them. Just attempting it is great fun, and a way to reacquaint yourself with these classics. The results can be some very special programming. I've only reported on nine of them here. Now you try some.

A Sample Musical Story Hour Program
Theme: Caldecott Award Winners
Ages: Pre-school and early elementary

1. Participation Game:

Five Little Ducks

Five little ducks went out to play,
  Over the hills far away.
Mother Duck cried,
  "Quack! Quack! Quack!"
And only four little ducks
  Came running back.

The children join in with the "quacks" and call out the number of ducks left on the mitt or flannelboard. Finish all verses by substituting four, three, two, one, and none. Then say:

No little ducks went out to play,
   Over the hills and far away.
Daddy Duck cried, "Quack! Quack!"
   And all the little ducks
Came running back

2. Musical Story:

Story: *Make Way For Ducklings* (McCloskey)

Music: "Colonel Bogey's March"

Musical Mood: A march to orchestrate the ducklings' march through the city streets.

3. Musical Story:

Story: *Finders Keepers* (Lipkind)

Music: Violin Concerto, third movement (Mendelssohn)

Musical Mood: Light and lively

Puppets: Two small dogs, one large dog, and a bone. Your puppeteers use simple movements acting out the story you're telling with the book in front of the stage.

4. Weston Woods Filmstrip:

Why Mosquitoes Buzz in People's Ears

5. Activity:

Coloring: A duckling or a dog.

Caldecott Winners for Parents and Children to Share (or for Storytelling)

The Randolph Caldecott Medal has been awarded annually since 1938 to the illustrator of the most distinguished American picture book for children:

Year	Title	Author	Illustrator
1938	*Animals of the Bible*	Fish	Lathrop
1939	*Mei Lei*	Handforth	Handforth
1940	*Abraham Lincoln*	d'Aulaire	d'Aulaire
1941	*They Were Strong and Good*	Lawson	Lawson
1942	*Make Way for Ducklings*	McCloskey	McCloskey
1943	*The Little House*	Burton	Burton
1944	*Many Moons*	Thurber	Slobodkin
1945	*Prayer for a Child*	Field	E. Jones
1946	*The Rooster Crows*	Petersham	Petersham
1947	*The Little Island*	MacDonald	Weisgard
1948	*White Snow, Bright Snow*	Tresselt	Duvoisin
1949	*The Big Snow*	Hader	Hader
1950	*Song of the Swallows*	Politi	Politi
1951	*The Egg Tree*	Milhous	Milhous
1952	*Finders Keepers*	Lipkind	Mordvinoff
1953	*The Biggest Bear*	Ward	Ward
1954	*Madeline's Rescue*	Bemelmans	Bemelmans
1955	*Cinderella*	Brown	Brown
1956	*Frog Went a Courtin'*	Langstaff	Rojankovsky
1957	*A Tree is Nice*	Udry	Simont
1958	*Time of Wonder*	McCloskey	McCloskey
1959	*Chanticleer and the Fox*	Cooney	Cooney
1960	*Nine Days to Christmas*	Ets	Ets
1961	*Baboushka and the Three Kings*	Robbins	Sidjakov
1962	*Once a Mouse*	Brown	Brown
1963	*The Snowy Day*	Keats	Keats
1964	*Where the Wild Things Are*	Sendak	Sendak
1965	*May I Bring a Friend?*	de Regniers	Montresor
1966	*Always Room for One More*	Nic Leodhas	Hogrogian
1967	*Sam, Bangs and Moonshine*	Ness	Ness
1968	*Drummer Hoff*	Emberley	Emberley
1969	*The Fool of the World and the Flying Ship*	Dayrell	Shulevitz
1970	*Sylvester and the Magic Pebble*	Steig	Steig

1971	*A Story, A Story*	Haley	Haley
1972	*One Fine Day*	Hogrogian	Hogrogian
1973	*The Funny Little Woman*	Mosel	Lent
1974	*Duffy and the Devil*	Zemach	Zemach
1975	*Arrow to the Sun*	McDermott	McDermott
1976	*Why Mosquitoes Buzz in People's Ears*	Aardema	Dillon
1977	*Ashanti to Zulu*	Musgrove	Dillon
1978	*Noah's Ark*	Spier	Spier
1979	*The Girl Who Loved Wild Horses*	Goble	Goble
1980	*Ox Cart Man*	Hall	Cooney
1981	*Fables*	Lobel	Lobel
1982	*Jumanji*	Van Allsburg	Van Allsburg
1983	*Shadow*	Cendrars	Brown
1984	*The Glorious Flight*	Provensen	Provensen
1985	*Saint George and the Dragon*	Hodges	Hyman
1986	*Polar Express*	Van Allsburg	Van Allsburg
1987	*Hey, Al*	Yorinks	Egielski
1988	*Owl Moon*	Yolen	Schoenherr

References

Cassette:

"Colonel Bogey's March." *Circus Calyope.* Gay 90s Village 5174-67.

Record Albums:

Beethoven, Ludwig van. Symphony no. 6, first, third, and fifth movements. *Ludwig van Beethoven, Symphony No. 6 in F, opus 68.* Arturo Toscanini and the NBC Symphony Orchestra. RCA Victor LM-1755.

"Dubula." *The World of Miriam Makeba.* RCA Victor LSP-2750.

Dvořák, Antonin. Symphony no. 5 (*New World* Symphony). *Dvořák—New World Symphony.* Philharmonic Symphony Orchestra of London. Westminster XWN-18295.

Gluck. "Dance of the Blessed Spirits. *Great Music for Relaxation.* RCA Victor LM-2800.

"Into Yam." *The World of Miriam Makeba.* RCA Victor LSP-2750.

Kabalevsky. "Galop." *Music to Have Fun By.* RCA Victor LSC-2813.

Liszt, Franz. "Grand Galop Chromatique." *Music to Have Fun By.* RCA Victor LSC-2813.

Mendelssohn, Felx. "On the Wings of Song." *Oistrakh.* David Oistrakh, violinist. Columbia ML 5096.

———. "Spring Song. *Popular Classics.* Volume 2. Morton Gould and his Orchestra. RCA VICS-1381.

———. Violin Concerto in E Minor, third movement. *Mendelssohn—Violin Concerto and Hebrides Overture.* Whitehall WH 20003.

Sousa, John Philip. "Washington Post March." *Semper Fidelis: The Marches of John Philip Sousa.* The Goldman Band. Harmony HL 7001.

"Sukiyaka." *Walt Disney Presents It's a Small World—18 Favorite Folk Songs.* Disneyland 1289.

Books:

Cendrars, Blaise. *Shadow.* Charles Scribner's Sons, 1982.

Goble, Paul. *The Girl Who Loved Wild Horses.* Bradbury Press, 1978.

Lipkind, William. *Finders Keepers.* Harcourt Brace Jovanovich, 1951.

McCloskey, Robert. *Make Way for Ducklings.* Viking, 1941.

McDermott, Gerald. *Arrow to the Sun: A Pueblo Indian Tale.* Viking, 1974.

Milhous, Katherine. *The Egg Tree.* Charles Scribner's Sons, 1950.

Mosel, Arlene. *The Funny Little Woman.* Dutton, 1972.

Steig, William. *Sylvester and the Magic Pebble.* Simon and Schuster, 1969.

Udry, Janice. *A Tree is Nice.* Harper and Row, 1956.

17.

Fables and Folk Tales

Rapunzel meets Debussy's "Girl with the Flaxen Hair" and other international pairings

Many classic folk tales, like "Rapunzel," lend themselves very well to a little musical interpretation. Here, you'll recall, Rapunzel's father takes some rampion from a witch for his sick wife. The witch insists he give her the child his wife is about to bear. As Rapunzel, and her hair, grow, the witch puts the beautiful child in a tower, and enters it via the ladder of cascading hair. The prince discovers the increasingly lovely girl, and visits via the same route. When the witch discovers this, she takes Rapunzel to the woods, then ambushes and blinds the prince. The lovers manage to find each other, and Rapunzel's tears fall on the prince's blind eyes and restore their sight. Off they go to the prince's kingdom, to live happily ever after.

Now that we have the European Community Concept, I guess I could be forgiven for bringing in a French composer— Claude Debussy— to use with this German story from the Brothers Grimm. Debussy's delicate and soft music, "The Girl with the Flaxen Hair," seems to me a natural and perfect choice for a girl with the wonderful long hair "as fine as spun gold."

The same *Andrew Lang Fairy Tale Treasury* provides "The Six Swans," another classic folk tale. Here the king becomes lost in the woods, and he meets a witch who makes some pretty rugged demands in exchange for showing him the way out. The king must marry the witch's daughter.

The king's previous marriage had resulted in seven children—six boys and a girl. He put them all in a lonely castle, fearing they would not be treated well by the new stepmother.

Sure enough, the stepmother wants all the king's attention and eventually finds the children, changing the boys into swans.

Their sister hides. Soon she learns that to break the spell she must not speak or laugh for six years, and must make six shirts out of star flowers for her brothers. The faithful sister determines to free them from the spell even if it costs her life.

The silent sister is married to a king who finds her, but his wicked mother takes their baby, hides it, and tells all that the wife has killed the child. Unable to speak and defend herself, she is shunned. After the second and third child meet the same fate, our heroine is sent to be burned at the stake—on the final day of the six years. At the last moment, the swans fly to her, flutter around her, and are changed back to their human form. Now she can speak the truth. She tells the king that his wicked mother has hidden the children and has unjustly accused her. The children are fetched, to the great delight of the king, and all is well once again.

Jean Sibelius composed a long, slow, mysterious piece called "The Swan of Tuonela" which fits the mood of 'The Six Swans" rather well. Both the music and the story have an aura of intrigue and mystery that complement one another. Sibelius succeeded in evoking musically the image of the swan moving in the water and the woods. It's altogether a rather interesting pairing of story and music.

Let's try matching a French story with a French composer this time. Charles Perrault's "Sleeping Beauty" is the tale. In this familiar story, the king and queen invite all the fairies except one to their daughter's christening feast. The king tries to make up for the oversight, but can't come up with a gold cover under a gold knife and fork for her, as he has for the others. Jealousy and rage fill the old fairy.

All the others present the child with their pleasant gifts, while the spiteful fairy vows that when the child is older she will prick her finger with a spindle and kill her. One of the other fairies comforts the parents by softening the effects of the spell. If the girl were to prick her finger, she would not die but sleep for 100 years ana then be awakened by a king's son.

At fifteen, the girl does indeed prick her finger on a spindle. The king lets her sleep in peace, but summons the good fairy, who promptly puts everyone to sleep except the king and queen.

Thorny briars grow around the castle and the sleeping beauty is quite forgotten. The hundred years pass, and the king dies. The newly reigning king's son hears the story and goes in search of the girl, forcing his way through the thick woods. Some say he kisses her, but it is not known for sure. Nevertheless, the end of her enchantment has come. That very evening (after eating) the marriage is celebrated.

I can't think of a more appropriate musical background for this sleepy story than Claude Debussy's "Reverie." The dreamy, romantic quality of the music reflects the 100 years that Sleeping Beauty has had to dream about her prince. The soft and quiet tones of the music create a mood for the slow passing of a century as the briars grow up around the silent castle. It is indeed a very good match of music and story. The popularized version of the melody is called "My Reverie," recorded by the Norman Luboff singers and many others.

Augusta Baker collected folk tales from all over the world in her 1955 anthology, *The Talking Tree and Other Stories*. One of them is the Norwegian classic, "East of the Sun and West of the Moon." In this story, a poor farmer trying to support his children gets an offer he can't refuse from a large white bear. If the bear can have the daughter, the farmer will receive great riches. Off the girl goes, riding on the bear's back.

The bear changes into human form at night, but the girl never sees his face. When the girl readies herself to return home to visit her family, the man-bear tells her not to let her mother talk to her alone. She tries to obey, but the mother gets her alone anyway and offers some advice. Light a candle, the mother says, and you will be able to see his face.

The advice seems harmless, so the candle is indeed lit. This ends the man-bear's chances to break the spell that he is under. Now he must go away, to a castle east of the sun and west of the moon, and marry a girl whose nose is three yards long.

Only through great efforts, travel, meetings with the winds, searching, and fast thinking is the girl finally able to locate her man, win him away from the long-nosed rival, and break all spells.

For such a Norwegian tale involving personified winds, trolls, and rugged countryside, a good Norwegian musical background is in order. Edvard Grieg's Piano Concerto in A Minor (first movement) offers an evocative musical feeling for all the wild landscape and weather and fictional characters of Norway. Of course, the world of folk tales is enormously wide and varied. You may wish to use an anthology of folk songs with a number of stories from around the world. Disney put out eighteen folk songs in a collection titled, *Walt Disney Presents "It's a Small World."* This collection includes "Frere Jacques" and "Alouette" from France, "Santa Lucia" from Italy, "Cielito Lindo" from Mexico, "Arirang" from Korea, "Kookaburra" from Australia, "Sukiyaka" from Japan, and others from all over. Any of these folk songs could be helpful with folk tale programs.

We have just scratched the surface here. The wide world of folk tales offers a real challenge for musical pairings.

A Sample Musical Story Hour Program
Theme: Fables and Folk Tales
Ages: 6–10

1. Musical Story:

Story:	"Rapunzel"
Music:	"The Girl With the Flaxen Hair" (Debussy)
Musical Mood:	Delicate and soft

2. Musical Story:

Story:	"Sleeping Beauty"
Music:	"Reverie" (Debussy)
Musical Mood:	Slow, dream-like, sleepy, romantic
Puppets:	A girl, a king, a prince, some fairies.

Since these are rather long stories, there is no need to add more to the program. This one is better for an audience of 6–9 years of age rather than pre-schoolers.

Other Folklore and Fairy Tale Books for Parents and Children to Share (or for Storytelling)

Andersen, Hans Christian. *Fairy Tales*. (Viking, 1981).

Asian Cultural Center. *Folk Tales from Asia for Children Everywhere*. Weatherhill, 1975.

Courlander, Harold. *A Treasury of African Folklore*. Crown, 1975.

Degh, Linda. *Folktales of Hungary*. University of Chicago Press, 1965.

Jacobs, Joseph. *Ardizonne's English Fairy Tales*. Deutsch, 1980.

Manning-Sanders, Ruth. *A Book of Ogres and Trolls*. Dutton, 1973.

Opie, Iona. *The Classic Fairy Tales*. Oxford University Press, 1974.

Parker, K. L. *Australian Legendary Tales*. Viking, 1966.

Pyle, Howard. *The Book of King Arthur*. Classic Publishing, 1970.

Sleigh, Barbara, reteller. *North of Nowhere: Stories and Legends from Many Lands*. Coward McCann, 1964.

Stoutenberg, Adrian. *American Tall Tales*. Viking, 1966.

Tales from the Arabian Nights. Translated by Richard F. Burton. Avenel, 1978.

White, Anne Terry, reteller. *Aesop's Fables*. Random House, 1964.

References

Record Albums:

Debussy, Claude. "The Girl with the Flaxen Hair." *The Lure of France*. Andre Kostelanetz and his Orchestra. Columbia CS 8111.

————. "Reverie." *The Lure of France.* Andre Kostelanetz and his Orchestra. Columbia CS 8111.

Greig, Edvard. Piano Concerto in A Minor. *The Great Romantic Piano concertos.* Philippe Entremont, pianist. Eugene Ormandy and the Philadelphia Orchestra. Columbia MG 32050.

Sibelius, Jean. "The Swan of Tuonela." *The Magnificent Sound of the Philadelphia Orchestra.* Eugene Ormandy, conductor. Columbia XSM 55824.

Walt Disney Presents It's a Small World—18 Favorite Folksongs. Disneyland 1289.

Books:

Baker, Augusta, editor. "East of the Sun and West of the Moon." *The Talking Tree and Other Stories.* Lippincott, 1955.

Grimm Brothers. "Rapunzel." *The Andrew Lang Fairy Tale Treasury.* Avenel Books, 1979.

"The Six Swans." *The Andrew Lang Fairy Tale Treasury.* Avenel Books, 1979.

"Sleeping Beauty." *The Arthur Rackham Fairy Book.* Crown, 1978.

18.

Orchestrating Dr. Seuss

Zany sounds for zany stories

Two of our favorite Dr. Seuss stories are lesser known tales from *The Sneetches and Other Stories:* "Too Many Daves" and "What Was I Scared Of?" In the first story—which works even better if you have a David or two in the audience—we learn that Mrs. McCave made the mistake of naming all twenty-three of her sons "Dave." When she realizes what a mistake it was, since they all come at once when she calls one, she thinks of all the names she *should* have used: Ziggy, Buffalo Bill, Biffalo Buff, Sir Michael Carmichael Zutt, Oliver Boliver Butt, etc.

The names never fail to elicit gales of laughter from four- and 5-year olds. To match such funny sounding names musically, a funny sounding instrument works well. Vivaldi's Concerto in G Minor for Bassoon (the opening movement) makes an excellent accompaniment. The bassoon is an unusual instrument, rather comical sounding, and this particular piece is upbeat and fitting for a humorous story. It sets the tone and the mood very well. Very few stories get such belly laughs as this one!

The second Seuss story is "What Was I Scared Of?" also from *The Sneetches* anthology. This is the story of a flying pair of pale green pants with nobody inside them. The pants terrify the small hero, by riding a bike near him, rowing a boat toward him, and even touching him while he tries to hide in a Snide bush. Our hero shrieks, yowls, and howls (Dr. Seuss was always good with verbs), but eventually befriends the pants and they end up as pals.

I spent two weeks asking people if anyone in their home owned a pair of pale green pants I could borrow to use with the story. No one had any such thing, until I found my daughter Jill had a pair of slacks in that shade, so I promptly "borrowed" them. We hung them over the edge of the puppet stage, shaking them throughout the story. What a challenge to find just the right music for this story! It needed music that could give the impression of empty pants jumping through the air and swaying spookily as if on a clothesline. Something a little spooky, but not heavily so. I finally found a piece—"Anitra's Dance" from Edvard Grieg's *Peer Gynt Suite*. There are violin parts that hop (in unison with the puppeteer working the pants) and sway (also in unison). Being a dance piece, the suggestion of movement is quite naturally built in.

Let's move from the scariness of the lime green pants with nobody in them, to a more peaceful and sleepy story—*Dr. Seuss' Sleep Book*. A yawn, like a cough, is quite catching. The Hinkle Horn Honkers have honked themselves out—a feeling not unknown to many of us, just expressed better. The Collapsable Frink collapses in a heap. By the end of the book, ninety-nine zillion, nine trillion and three people have nodded off to sleep.

We need something dreamy for this story. The Brahms Lullaby is an obvious choice for a book about falling asleep. A less obvious selection is Claude Debussy's "Prelude to the Afternoon of a Faun." This quiet, poetic, and sensitive piece makes a nice background for Seuss's sleepy critters.

Dr. Seuss can also wake us up with a boastful story like "I Can Lick Thirty Tigers Today." By the end of the story, our boastful hero drops the thirty down to one, or so. For a peppy and appropriate musical counterpoint, The Dukes of Dixieland have a great version of "Tiger Rag." (There are many good versions of this "Hold That Tiger" available).

One of Dr. Seuss's stories which has a deeper meaning or moral than most of the whimsical tales is *Horton Hears a Who*. The microscopic "who," which Horton the elephants hears, is so tiny that no one else can hear its voice. Horton has to search through three million flowers to locate the Who Village. The ever faithful elephant saves his tiny friends from harm and preaches, "A person's a person no matter how small."

I looked for something to go with the three million flowers for this story. I found two pieces of music which are equally "flowerful." The first is Johann Strauss's "Voices of Spring." The tune (if not the title) is familiar to most people, and the image of fields of flowers is evoked very strongly.

Another good choice, even more familiar, is Tchaikovsky's "Waltz of the Flowers" from the *Nutcracker* Suite. There are many stories with which this popular classic can be used whenever you want to call forth a musical picture of fields and flowers.

Of course, the other famous example of Horton's faithfulness is *Horton Hatches the Egg*. In this one he babysits an egg for a self-liberated mother bird who flies south for awhile and stays there. Meanwhile, Horton stays on the egg through all kinds of bad weather and hardships. The elephant bird which hatches seems like a just reward for such elephantine faithfulness.

Delving a little out of the familiar, the recommended choice of composer and music for this story is a bit unusual. I like Haydn for this one—in particular, the second movement of his Symphony no. 101 (the *Clock* Symphony). Writing so many symphonies, Haydn settled into a consistently dignified and calm style, without the need for theatrics found in the symphonies of so many composers. This symphony seems to reflect the calm determination of our unflappable elephant. The second movement adds an unusual element—the tick-tock rhythm of a clock-like sound—a steady light background which goes well with the hatching of the egg. It reinforces the memorable image of Horton, sitting through the snowstorm, faithfully hatching the egg.

Many of the Seuss stories reflect a pure fanciful quality of ridiculous situations made almost believable by the plot, and even funnier by the rhyme.

Green Eggs and Ham falls into this category as does *The Cat In the Hat*. For stories like these, once again, I look for an odd or unfamiliar sounding instrument featured in a light and upbeat piece of music. Mozart offers several possibilities. The opening allegro movement of his Bassoon Concerto in B-flat Major like the earlier mentioned Vivaldi piece, gives the odd sound and light pace needed. The more easily located Horn Concertos

(French horns) also offer an unusual sound—not quite as Seuss-like as a bassoon, but still effective. The opening allegro movements of his Horn Concertos no. 1 and no. 4 are both good choices. Of course, you can find good old Boots Randolph anywhere and use the unusual and upbeat sounds of "Yakety Sax" just as well, but this kind of introduction to Mozart at an early age may be important to some of your listeners and worth your effort.

Leroy Anderson's "The Waltzing Cat" is a violin piece where the violins "meow" like a cat, which is also an effective background for *The Cat in the Hat*.

A Sample Musical Story Hour Program
Theme: Dr. Seuss
Ages: Pre-school and early elementary

1. Musical Story:

Story: "Too Many Daves" (from *The Sneetches and Other Stories*)

Music: Concerto in G Minor for Bassoon, first movement (Vivaldi)

Musical   Unusual, light, and humorous
Mood:

2. Activity:

Ask how many Davids there are in the audience. Then ask the whole group to pretend they're *all* named Dave and ask them to answer your questions, all together at the same time. ("Don't raise your hands, just *answer!*")

"What did you have for breakfast today, Dave?"

"What's your favorite t.v. show, Dave?"

"Hey, Dave, what do you do in school all day?"

The cacophony of answers will usually get some laughs and make the point of "Too Many Daves"!

3. Musical Story:

Story: *Green Eggs and Ham* (two people read it as a conversation)

Music: Bassoon Concerto in B-flat Major (Mozart). If the Mozart is too hard to locate, you could use "Yakety Sax" by Boots Randolph.

Musical Mood: Unusual, light, and humorous.

4. Participation Game:

Five Mice and the Fat Cat

Five little mice
    Came out to play,
Gathering crumbs along the way.
Here comes the cat
    Fat and fast, fat and fast.
Four little mice
    Came out to play.

(Finish, using three, two, one. Have the children call out the numbers.)

5. Musical Story:

Story: *The Cat in the Hat*

Music: "The Waltzing Cat" (Leroy Anderson)

Musical Mood: Evocative of a cat, humorous

Other Dr. Seuss Books for Parents and Children to Share (or for Storytelling):

Bartholew and the Oobleck. Random House, 1949.

The Cat in the Hat Comes Back. Beginner Books, 1958.

Five Hundred Hats of Bartholemew Cubbins. Random House, 1938.

Happy Birthday to You. Random House, 1959.

Hop on Pop. Beginner Books, 1963.

How the Grinch Stole Christmas. Random House, 1957.

Hunches in Bunches. Random House, 1982.

If I Ran the Zoo. Random House, 1950.

Yertle the Turtle and Other Stories. Random House, 1958.

References

Cassettes:

Haydn, Franz Joseph. Symphony no. 101, second movement, CBS MP-39025.

Vivaldi, Antonio. Concerto in G Minor for Bassoon. *Vivaldi: Concertos for Diverse Instruments.* The Bach Guild CHM 16.

Record Albums:

Anderson, Leroy. "The Waltzing Cat." *Fiddle Faddle.* Arthur Fiedler and the Boston Pops. RCA Victor LM 2638.

Brahms, Johannes. Lullaby. *Nightfall.* Carmen Dragon and the Capitol Symphony Orchestra. Capitol SP 8575.

Debussy, Claude. "Prelude to the Afternoon of a Faun." *The Magnificent Sound of the Philadelphia Orchestra.* Eugene Ormandy, conductor. Columbia XSM 55824.

Grieg, Edvard. "Anitra's Dance." *The Magnificent Sound of the Philadelphia Orchestra.* Eugene Ormandy, conductor. Columbia XSM 55824.

Mozart, Wolfgang. Bassoon Concerto in B-flat Major. *Mozart—Music for Winds and Brass.* Murray Hill S-4364.

———. Horn Concertos no. 1 and 4. *Mozart—Music for Winds and Brass.* Murray Hill S-4364.

Strauss, Johann. "Voices of Spring." *The Magnificent Sound of the Philadelphia Orchestra*. Eugene Ormandy, conductor. Columbia XSM 55824.

Tchaikovsky, Peter. "Waltz of the Flowers." *The Nutcracker Suite*. Homburg State Orchestra. Coronet CXS 20.

"Tiger Rag." *At the Jazz Band Ball*. The Dukes of Dixieland. Vik LX-1025.

"Yakety Sax." *Boots Randolph's Yakety Sax*. Monument SLP 18002.

Books (by Dr. Seuss):

The Cat in the Hat. Random House, 1957.

Dr. Seuss' Sleep Book. Random House, 1962.

Green Eggs and Ham. Random House, 1960.

Horton Hatches the Egg. Random House, 1940.

Horton Hears a Who. Random House, 1954.

I Can Lick 30 Tigers Today—and Other Stories. Random House, 1969.

"Too Many Daves." *The Sneetches and Other Stories*. Random House, 1961.

"What Was I Scared Of?" *The Sneetches and Other Stories*. Random House, 1961.

19.

Orchestrating Bill Peet

Circus music and marches for
Peet's delightful animals

I discovered Bill Peet back in 1964 while I was looking for a book to take for storytelling at school visits. We were trying to go to every classroom in every school in the area surrounding our branch. Bowen Branch was in a Mexican-American section of Detroit, near the Ambassador Bridge leading to Windsor, Canada. That particular section of town was teeming with children, and there were plenty of schools to be visited.

Peet came out with *Ella* in 1964 and it was love at first sight. The idea of using music with the story didn't occur to me for another couple of decades. It was just wonderful to find a story which could be counted on to delight every class visited. Back then I tended to stick with what worked for me, and probably set a world's record for telling one story so many times.

As Spencer Shaw mentioned in his 1958 article ("Recorded Magic for Story Hours"), the storytelling is always the main thing, and the music you might use is an aid. Storytelling skills have always been the primary necessity. By going from classroom to classroom with *Ella* in so many schools, I eventually learned when and how to pause, raise my voice, slow down, gesture, give a knowing smirk, frown, smile, ask a question.

Many years later, I still find that Peet's story of the spoiled elephant who runs away from the circus has a timeless ability to delight children. Ella runs away because of the gross indignity of being made to push the circus wagons out of the mud in a rainstorm. Captured by a farmer, she finds herself forced to do even worse work for a year—feeding pigs, mowing grass, collecting firewood, gathering eggs, and picking apples. Seeing the smoke of the circus train after a year, Ella crashes through the side of the barn in order to escape and run back home. Such a story would appeal to any child.

An interesting way to use music with this tale is to try authentic circus calliope music at the beginning and end, leaving the dreary events of Ella's farm life to silence. The trick here, however, is to find circus calliope music. I remember going up to the manager of the record store at one of our large Miami malls and asking for calliope music, to which the perky young woman replied, "What's calliope music?"

Well, that dated me enough. I didn't feel the need to tell her I remembered the *tents* that Ringling Brothers and Barnum and Bailey used to bring to Philadelphia for their performances when I was a kid—with real calliopes!

More ventures into other record stores were equally unproductive, until, I happened to be visiting the John Ringling Circus Museum in Sarasota, Florida. In their gift shop they had several excellent cassette tapes of authentic calliope music for sale. "Circus Calyope" contains such old standards as "The Man on the Flying Trapeze," "The Jolly Cobbler," "The Jolly Coppersmith," "Margie," and "In the Good Old Summer Time." The company which puts these out was listed on the blurb:

> Paul R. Eakins's Gay 90s Village, Inc.
> Box 569
> Sikeston, Missouri 63801

The address of the museum is:
> Ringling Circus Museum
> 5401 Bayshore Road
> Sarasota, Florida 34243

Since calliope music is so difficult to find, you might want to contact either place to see about purchasing some. It's terrific for *Ella* or others of Peet's circus stories such as *Randy's Dandy Lions,* another favorite.

Encore for Eleanor gives us another elephant heroine. Eleanor is too old to perform in the circus anymore, so they ship her to the zoo instead. Here the rejected pachyderm hides from public view until her hidden talents are discovered. Picking up a piece of charcoal, Eleanor sketches a clown and a lion, to the amazement of the zookeeper. She is soon the star attraction of the zoo, just as she had been at the circus, drawing large crowds to see her pictures.

I've found several Sousa marches that give the same circus effect as calliope music. "The Thunderer," "The Washington Post March," "El Capitan," and "Semper Fidelis" all work well with these circus stories, and they are far easier to find than calliope music.

Peet's animals aren't all in the circus. *Merle, the High Flying Squirrel* is a common park squirrel who longs to go out west and see the giant redwoods. He starts his trek west by walking on telephone wires. He tries to free a child's kite from the wires when a storm blows him and the kite in the general direction of the redwoods. A tornado takes Merle the rest of the way.

For this trek over wires and through the air I like to use a piece by Gounod called "The Funeral March of a Marionette." You probably know it as the theme song for the television series "Alfred Hitchcock Presents." It has a quality that suggests marching or traveling which fits very well.

Some of Peet's stories have serious overtones, like *The Gnats of Knotty Pine*. The senseless killing of animals by hunters is Peet's target here. None of the animals can do anything to stop the mindless hunting, except the lowly gnats who band together and attack the men, driving them away.

This story needs no music until the ending when "The Flight of the Bumble Bee" adds some surprise, excitement, and a feeling of justice and victory for the underdog.

Cyrus the Unsinkable Sea Serpent, another lovable Peet hero, is challenged by a shark to sink a ship. Cyrus is too good-hearted though, and finds himself protecting the *Primrose* and its crew instead. He helps them overcome lack of breeze, a storm, and a pirate attack.

Debussy's *La Mer (The Sea)* offers some nice mood background for this story. The unpredictable waves and ever-changing music go hand in hand.

Some of Peet's stories are just plain fun, with no underdogs or social issues. One of his best is 1959's *Hubert's Hair Raising Adventure*. Here we could use some humorous music, not necessarily classical. I like Boots Randolph's saxophone versions of "Charlie Brown," "Cacklin' Sax," and "If You've Got the Money, Honey, I've Got the Time." In this purely fun category, you could also include The *Whingdingdilly* about the witch who turns Scamp, the dog, into a mixture of camel, rhino, giraffe, zebra, and others.

Orchestrating Bill Peet can be a tremendous amount of fun, whether you're using classical music, jazz, or something else. You might enjoy venturing out on your own, looking for the perfect combinations. Another helpful thing about Peet books is that the pictures are large and clear enough to be seen from a distance, so they lend themselves to being seen by all children in whatever room you're in.

A Sample Musical Story Hour Program
Theme: Bill Peet Stories
Ages: Pre-school and early elementary

1. Participation Game:

Elephant Song

One elephant went out to play,
Out on a spider's web one day.
He had such E-NORMOUS fun,
He called for another elephant to come.

(Keep placing one more elephant on your velcro mitt, or flannel board, until all five are on. Say or sing five times, substituting two, three, four, and five in place of one in the verse.)

2. Musical Story:

Story: *Ella*

Music: "The Jolly Coppersmith" or any similar circus calliope music.

Musical
Mood: Authentic circus music.

Puppets: An elephant, a farmer, a dog, a hen, several
             pigs, a clown, and a giraffe

3. Musical Story:

Story: *Merle, the High Flying Squirrel*

Music: "Funeral March of a Marionette" (Gounod)

Musical   Suggestive of walking or marching.
Mood:

Puppets: A squirrel

4. Film:

If you can afford to rent Dumbo from the Disney people,
Peet was one of the animators of this original Disney classic.

Other Bill Peet Titles for Parents and Children to Share (or for Storytelling):

The Ant and the Elephant. Houghton Mifflin, 1972.

Buford the Little Bighorn. Houghton Mifflin, 1967.

Caboose Who Got Loose. Houghton Mifflin, 1971.

Chester, the Worldly Pig. Houghton Mifflin, 1965.

Cowardly Clyde. Houghton Mifflin, 1979.

The Luckiest One of All. Houghton Mifflin, 1982.

No Such Things. Houghton Mifflin, 1983.

Pamela Camel. Houghton Mifflin, 1984.

The Pinkish, Purplish, Bluish Egg. Houghton Mifflin, 1963.

Smokey. Houghton Mifflin, 1962.

The Wump World. Houghton Mifflin, 1970.

Zella, Zack and Zodiac. Houghton Mifflin, 1985.

References

Cassette:

Circus Calyope. Paul R. Eakin's Gay 90s Village, Inc. 5174-67.

Record Albums:

Debussy, Claude, "La Mer." *Afternoon of a Faun, Daphnis and Chloe no. 2, and La Mer*. Eugene Ormandy and the Philadelphia Orchestra. Columbia ML 5397.

Gounod. "Funeral March of a Marionette." *Music to Have Fun By*. RCA Victor LSC-2813.

Rimsky-Korsakov, Nikolai. "Flight of the Bumble Bee." *Music to Have Fun By*. RCA Victor LSC-2813.

Sousa, John Philip. *Semper Fidelis: The Marches of John Philip Sousa*. The Goldman Band. Harmony HL 7001.

"Yakety Sax." *Boots Randolph's Yakety Sax*. Monument SLP 18002.

Books (by Bill Peet):

Cyrus the Unsinkable Sea Serpent. Houghton Mifflin, 1975.

Ella. Houghton Mifflin, 1964.

Encore for Eleanor. Houghton Mifflin, 1981.

The Gnats of Knotty Pine. Houghton Mifflin, 1975.

Hubert's Hair-Raising Adventure. Houghton Mifflin, 1959.

Merle the High-Flying Squirrel. Houghton Mifflin, 1974.

Randy's Dandy Lions. Houghton Mifflin, 1964.

Article:

Shaw, Spencer. "Recorded Magic for Story Hours." *Top of the News*, October 1958.

20.

Moonlight Sonatas

Using "Clair de Lune" and the *Moonlight* Sonata with stories about the moon

I have a special interest in books with a little moonlight in them, as well as an inclination to find stories to use with the opening of Beethoven's *Moonlight* Sonata or Debussy's "Clair de Lune." The delightful thing about using these two pieces is that you know that everybody will love hearing them, and that they are so famous that finding them presents no problem.

If you've never specifically tried to locate moon stories, you may be surprised at how many you can turn up if you look. You really don't need more than those two moon-music classics to go with all of them.

Perfection! Frank Asch's charming story, *Moongame*, meeting the *Moonlight* Sonata. If any combination perfectly illustrates what I'm trying to say in this book, this is it. Even if you don't have an audience of children at this moment, grab the book, get the music, and read yourself a story—you'll see right away what I've been driving at all this time.

In case you don't have a copy of *Moongame* handy, I'll briefly describe it. Asch's Bear decides to play hide-and-seek with the moon. He hides in a tree, but, peeking out, he sees the moon has found him. The moon seems to take its turn hiding, gliding behind a large black cloud, until Bear and his little friends eventually find it again.

This is a sensitive, gorgeously illustrated story. If a puppeteer could come up with a squirrel, a skunk, a duck, a bird, a turtle, and a deer—to go with the bear and a makeshift moon—turn out the lights, turn on the *Moonlight* Sonata and wow! All the ingredients for an absolutely dynamite children's program are there: a storyteller, a beautiful book, a few simple puppets, one prop (the moon), dramatic lighting. You can create a magical and unforgettable experience bringing books, music and children together.

There are so many excellent versions of the *Moonlight* Sonata available, but I do have one favorite. The French pianist, Phillipe Entremont, seems to be at home with the most sensitive and romantic of music. He's really a natural for this one.

Mooncake is another Frank Asch book that could take either of these pieces as background music. In this one, Bear and his friend, the bird, wish they could go to the moon to eat some of it. Bear builds a rocket, falls asleep in it, and when he wakes up, thinks he has arrived. He eats some snow, which he thinks is mooncake, returns to the rocket, and falls asleep again. By the time he awakens this time, he believes he is back on earth. When the bird asks him how the moon tasted, Bear assures him that it was just fine.

A less fanciful tale, involving a real slice of American history, with just a touch of the moon at the end, is Leo Politi's wonderful Caldecott Award winner, *The Song of the Swallows*. Here we meet Old Julian, the bell ringer and gardener in the mission at Capistrano. We also meet his young friend, Juan, who lives nearby. Julian tells Juan about the brothers of Saint Francis, the building of the early missions, the skills the Indians learned there, and about Father Junipero Serro. The old man also tells the boy how the swallows return to the area each year on Saint Joseph's Day.

Juan begins creating a garden of his own, at his home, in hope of attracting some swallows. As he works he hums the song, "La Golondrina" ("The Swallow") which he had learned in school. The words and music are reprinted in the book.

In Spencer Shaw's 1958 article, "Recorded Magic for Story Hours," he recommended using this song with the story. Perhaps you can sing or play the piano or make a tape of someone else playing it. If you can find a live pianist and have a piano, this is surely a nice accompaniment to offer.

The story ends quietly on a moonlit night. Juan is looking out his window at two swallows that have come to his new garden and are sleeping on his rose vine. This could be a nice spot to bring in the *Moonlight* Sonata briefly and turn the volume down in a fade-out as the story ends.

This story is especially appropriate for California storytellers, of course, but it is just as appropriate here in North Miami because our library is located about a mile from an authentic Spanish monastery built in 1141! The Monastery of Saint Bernard de Clairvaux had originally been built in Segovia, Spain, during the reign of King Alphonso VII, and named "The Monastery of Our Lady, Queen of Angels." Cisterian monks occupied the monastery for nearly 700 years. During a social revolution, the buildings were seized and sold, converted into a granary and stable.

In 1925, William Randolph Hearst purchased the buildings for $500,000, planning to ship them to his California estate, San Simeon. The stones were packed with hay in 11,000 wooden crates ready to be shipped to the U.S. However, a hoof-and-mouth disease outbreak in Segovia caused the U.S. Department of Agriculture to ban the shipment since the hay might have brought in the organism. The hay was burned, and the stones were carelessly repacked, with their numbers scrambled. To put them together correctly would be like doing the world's largest and most expensive jigsaw puzzle. The stones stayed in a Brooklyn warehouse for twenty-six years, as Hearst developed financial problems.

In 1952, they were purchased by Messrs. W. Edgemon and R. Moss and brought to our neighboring city, North Miami Beach, to be assembled as a tourist attraction, a herculean task which took nineteen months. In 1964, the Cloisters were purchased by the Episcopal Diocese of South Florida. Church services, weddings, and sightseeing are popular at this historic spot.

This magnificent monastery makes a natural tie-in for *The Song of the Swallows* for all of the local libraries in our area. We only offer pelicans, seagulls and egrets here—no swallows—but we can claim an authentic Spanish monastery!

This story is told in part to encourage you to identify and use local tie-ins with books and accompanying music. It adds enormous interest to bring in a little history, local color or background to your storytelling program.

Returning to a more fanciful moon story now, there is a Br'er Rabbit story called "The Moon in the Mill Pond." In this, Br'er Rabbit again escapes the clutches of Br'er Fox and Br'er Wolf with some fast talking. He tells the menacing duo that he's on his way to catch the sumptuous and plentiful fish in the mill pond. Having bought some time, the little rabbit thinks fast when he sees the reflection of the moon in the water. He tells them that the moon fell in the pond and there won't be any fishing possible until they get it out of there. Off they go to fetch a net, and into the deep water go Br'er Fox and Br'er Wolf. Off to safety goes Br'er Rabbit.

I think the *Moonlight* Sonata and "Clair de Lune" are both a little too romantic for such a down-to-earth bunny. Henry Mancini's "Moon River," in a light instrumental version, seems like a better choice. Even something with a little more bounce, like Glenn Miller's old classic "Moonlight Serenade," would do well here.

Robert McCloskey's *Time of Wonder* presents still another visit from the moon. The fearsome roar of a New England hurricane causes a fearful night for the family inside the house. As they walk around with flashlights inside, they finally see the welcome full moon over the tips of the tall trees, bringing a promise that the storm will soon be over. The wind dies down to a lullaby in the spruce branches as the clouds disappear and the family falls asleep in the bright moonlight.

This is another sequence where you could well use the storm and clearing sequence in Beethoven's *Pastoral* Symphony. The sonata would also be nice as a short breaker between the storm music and the "sunnier" clearing music of the symphony. The three Beethoven sections—the storm, the sonata (just a little) and the passing of the storm—make a creative combination.

Phyllis Root came out with an interesting moon story in 1985 called *Moon Tiger*. This fanciful tale of sibling rivalry and fantasy starts off with a definitely earthy touch. Jessica Ellen, age seven, is jealous and angry because her mother yelled at her for not wanting to read a story to her little four-year-old brother. Jessica Ellen's mind takes her away from her troubles, into a dreamy fantasy concerning the arrival of her friend the moon tiger, leaping across the moonbeams and through her bedroom window. Naturally the girl jumps on his back and they fly away! They search for polar bears at the North Pole. They fly to Africa and see a real hippopotamus.

When the two world travelers finally fly back to the house, Jessica Ellen shows little brother Michael to the animal, who kindly offers, "Do you want me to eat him?" Tempting! Jessica thinks it over a long time before refusing the offer because her parents might be upset. Besides, Michael is fun and nice sometimes.

Perhaps a less than classical approach, with a little world-traveling touch, would be better for this "flight of fancy" with the moon tiger. How about an instrumental version of "Moonlight on the Ganges"? I found this on an album called *The New Ebb Tide* by the Frank Chacksfield Orchestra, and it seemed to add a nice touch. "Moon River," Henry Mancini's popular song, is also available on this album in an instrumental version which works well.

A classical piece which does offer a uniquely appropriate tone to this story would be one that you will immediately recognize as "Twinkle, Twinkle, Little Star." What it really is is the second movement of Haydn's *Surprise* Symphony, or Symphony no. 94. This is one of Haydn's best known and most easily found symphonies. The "Twinkle, Twinkle" movement is a gorgeously orchestrated piece of music, and the stars theme, familiar to all who hear it, fits in well with the story of the little girl and the tiger flying through the starlit sky around the world.

Whether you use these particular celestial stories or any of the many others available, it's a rather special challenge to match them with some moon music—classical, swing, or popular. The moon has fascinated people for centuries, and it certainly provides us with the opportunity for plenty of magical moments in our telling of tales.

A Sample Musical Story Hour Program
Theme: The Moon (and the Heavens)
Ages: Pre-school and early elementary

1. Participation Game:

Angels

Five little angels dressed in white,
Trying to get to heaven
On the end of a kite.
The kite broke and down they all fell.

But don't get excited,
Don't lose your head,
Instead of going to heaven,
They all went to bed!

(The next verses follow four, three, two, and one little angels, as the children call out the numbers left on your fingers or flannelboard.)

2. Musical Story:

Story: *Moongame* (Frank Asch)

Music: *Moonlight* Sonata, first movement (Beethoven)

Musical Mood: Quiet, beautiful, sensitive

3. Musical Story:

Story: *Mooncake* (Frank Asch)

Music: "Clair de Lune" (Debussy)

Musical Mood: Quiet, beautiful, and sensitive

4. Activity:

Coloring.
    Draw and photocopy the moon and some stars, or a character from your stories with the moon in the background.

References

Cassettes:

Haydn, Franz Joseph. Symphony no. 94. Leonard Bernstein and the New York Philharmonic Orchestra. Columbia MT 32101.

Miller, Glenn. "Moonlight Serenade." *Glenn Miller and His Orchestra*. SAAR 3865.

Record Albums:

Beethoven, Ludwig van. Sonata no. 14. *Greatest Hits for the Piano*. Philippe Entremont. Columbia M 31406.

————. Symphony no. 6. Arturo Toscanini and the NBC Symphony Orchestra. RCA Victor LM 1755.

Debussy, Claude. "Clair de Lune." *Greatest Hits for the Piano*. Philippe Entremont. Columbia M 31406.

Mancini, Henry. "Moon River." *The New Ebb Tide*. Frank Chacksfield and His Orchestra. London SP 44053.

"Moonlight on the Ganges." *The New Ebb Tide*. Frank Chacksfield and His Orchestra. London SP 44053.

Books:

Asch, Frank. *Mooncake*. Prentice-Hall, 1983.

————. *Moongame*. Prentice-Hall, 1984.

McCloskey, Robert. *Time of Wonder*. Viking, 1957.

Palmer, Marilyn, reteller. "The Moon in the Millpond." In *Walt Disney's Uncle Remus Stories*. Simon and Schuster, 1946.

Politi, Leo. *Song of the Swallows*. Charles Scribner's, 1946.

Root, Phyllis. *Moon Tiger*. Holt, Rinehart and Winston, 1985.

Article:

Shaw, Spencer. "Recorded Magic for Story Hours." *Top of the News*, October 1958.

21.

Russians

A little "glasnost" from Slobodkina, Tchaikovsky, Rimsky-Korsakov, and others

Esphyr Slobodkina was born in Cheliabinsk, Russia and is celebrating her eightieth birthday in 1988 at her home in Hallandale, Florida. In between she authored and illustrated twenty children's books and became a world-renowned abstract artist. Her most famous book is the classic, *Caps for Sale* from 1940.

I recently drove to Hallandale to pick her up for an appearance at our North Miami Public Library. We were having her come to speak to children and parents about her stories, her art, her tapestries, and her hand-made dolls. We were also surprising her with a puppet show based on another of her books, *The Wonderful Feast* (1954). I consider this to be her finest book, and she later mentioned that it's *her* favorite as well. This story has more depth than the others, and has been the subject of letters of praise. Finding music to match its depth is a real challenge.

The Wonderful Feast starts with Farmer Jones giving an ample measure of feed to his horse, Spotty. The horse eats all he needs and goes to sleep. While Spotty sleeps, the little she-goat Nanny walks into the shed, sees the leftovers and joyfully exclaims, "My, oh, my! What a wonderful feast I'm going to have!" She eats all she needs, and goes on her way.

The red hen, Strawberry, is the next visitor to the shed. She sees the leftover food and excitedly calls her ten chicks to partake in a wonderful feast. A solitary mouse spots the few remaining grains on the floor and has still another feast, filling himself completely. Finally, an ant looking for winter supplies comes in, sees the last remaining grain of feed on the floor and

143

thankfully mutters, "My, oh, my! What a wonderful feast I'm going to have."
You can enjoy this simply as a well-told story or you can find deeper meaning in it about sharing the world's resources or our personal resources. I consider it a profound story, and therefore I wanted a musical background with the depth to match it.

I found a piece by the Russian-Jewish composer Anton Rubinstein, which seemed to match extremely well with the story by this Russian-Jewish author-illustrator. The piece is "Kamenoi Ostrow," a haunting piece which has been said to depict a conception of heaven. The original "Kamenoi Ostrow" was a set of twenty-four piano pieces and refers to Stone Island, a Russian palace on an island in the Neva River. Number twenty-two of the twenty-four, "Reva Angelique," is the most popular piece and has become known, erroneously, as "Kamenoi Ostrow."

I think the blending of the story and music is unusually good. If the effect is too heavy for some people, a nice background of balalaika music is just as fine. Occasionally though, I like to try for a very special blending.

Anton Rubinstein died in 1894, a year after one of his students, Peter Ilich Tchaikovsky, died in St. Petersburg. As a child, the same deep feeling for music that comes through in "Kamenoi Ostrow" was growing in Tchaikovsky. At six, already fluent in German and French, the prodigy cut himself on a window pane broken during his absorbed drumming of a tune on the window with his fingernails. Despite such early intensity, which carried Tchaikovsky to some fervent musical heights later, I think his less frenetic waltzes are more appropriate for Slobodkina's stories.

Caps for Sale, the classic which has been retold many times on television by Bob Keeshan (Captain Kangaroo) is much lighter than *The Wonderful Feast.* I think its light exuberance can be matched by something like the waltz from Tchaikovsky's Serenade for Strings.

Caps for Sale introduces us to Pezzo the Peddler, the little Charlie Chaplinesque man who wears a black and white checkered hat beneath four tan caps, four brown caps, four blue caps, and four red ones. All the caps are for sale except the black and white one. The irreverent monkeys in the tree like the caps too, and they help themselves to one each, scampering up the tree with their bounty. It is only after much coaxing and complaining that the mischievous monkeys finally return the caps so that the peddler can continue his efforts to sell the pile, now safely back upon his head.

There are two sequels to *Caps for Sale*, *Pezzo the Peddler and the Seven Silly Thieves* and *Pezzo the Peddler and the Circus Elephant*. In these two stories, poor Pezzo runs into more irreverent folks who take his pile of caps.

In the first, thieves reach out of their jail cell windows to take the caps, and it is only after much frustrated effort that he gets the thieves to throw them back out. A fire engine clangs by and people shout, "Where's the fire?" Quick-witted Pezzo shouts back, "The thief's cap is on fire," and all the caps come flying out again.

In the second story Pezzo's caps are removed by a circus elephant and distributed to all the performers. Poor Pezzo sulks again, until the big boss of the circus finds him and offers Pezzo a job in the circus—balancing caps, which no one else was able to do.

Sticking with my match of Slobodkina and Tchaikovsky, I suggest the lively waltz from *Eugene Onegin* for either of these amusing and delightful tales.

Slobodkina's *Billy the Condominium Cat* definitely reflects her "Florida period"! Here we have another lively story, but this one slows down to a weary finale. When Billy and his aging owner, Bianca, were young and living in New Hampshire, there were kids all around and plenty of activity. When three rambunctious nephews visit Florida, the activity picks up again, with trips to the beach and Disney World. The old woman and her cat are quite worn out after the week's visit. "That was very nice," sighs Bianca, as she sinks into a comfortable chair and closes her eyes.

I like a combination by Tchaikovsky for this story. *The Nutcracker* Suite provides us with both a lively "Waltz Finale" and a sleepy, dreamy "Apotheosis" for the exhausted scene at the story's end.

For a final Slobodkina story I like another Russian concoction—this time Tchaikovsky and Rimsky-Korsakov. *Pinky and the Petunias* follows the escapades of a little kitten named Pinky who riles all the neighbors with his annoying habit of eating their petunias. No amount of scolding seems to stop this practice. Finally, a bee inside a flower stings the kitten's nose, breaking the habit of eating petunias forever. Could there be a much more obvious musical background as "The Waltz of the Flowers" followed suddenly by "The Flight of the Bumblebee"?

Esphyr Slobodkina represents an era of children's literature when charm, taste, and good storytelling prevailed. I feel honored to know her, and I take special pleasure in matching her stories with composers from her own native Russia. Like so many of the great old authors, however, most of her books have been allowed to go out of print. Some of your libraries will be fortunate enough to still have them around. For those of us who have been around long enough, we realize the problem of such outstanding picture books from years past not being in print today.

Sample Musical Story Hour Program
Theme: Russians

1. Musical Story:

Story:	*Caps for Sale* (Scholastic Co. has a useful oversize edition available, excellent for storytelling.)
Music:	Waltz from Serenade for Strings (Tchaikovsky)
Musical Mood:	Light, cheerful, upbeat
Activity:	Since the peddler of caps has many angry responses trying to get the monkeys to return his caps, it can be fun to have the children act out each one: shaking his finger at the monkeys, shaking both fists, stomping one foot, jumping up and down, throwing his last remaining cap on the ground. You could ask the youngsters, after the story, what *they* do when *they* get mad.

Game: "Monkey See, Monkey Do." The story could be
        considered an example of "Monkey See, Mon-
        key Do." Pezzo's final act of frustration—slam-
        ming his only remaining cap to the ground—is
        the one angry action he takes that works. All the
        monkeys see this and soon throw their caps,
        which they had taken off his head, to the
        ground as well. Pezzo picks up his caps and goes
        on his way yelling, "Caps for sale. Fifty cents a
        cap."

        You can explain the saying, "Monkey See,
        Monkey Do," and lead the group through all
        kinds of fun activities, having them do whatever
        they see you do—jumping, turning in circles,
        shaking your arms, etc.

Activity: If you use the oversize edition, or if you make a
            flannel board version of Pezzo and his thirteen
            caps, you could have the children slowly count
            the caps, aloud, one by one.

2. Musical Story:

Story: *The Wonderful Feast*

Music: "Kamenoi Ostrow" (Rubinstein)

Musical
Mood: Thoughtful, deep, profound, suggestive of the
         beauty of the day and the farm

Puppets: A farmer, a horse, a goat, a hen, chicks (Wizard
           of Ahhs' Monkey Mitt chicks are good for this.
           You can wrap each of the five tiny chicks around
           with a thin wire, leaving twelve inches with
           which to hold them up to the puppet stage),
           and an ant. (The latter is very difficult to find.
           We finally cut up a rubber spider!)

Song: "Old MacDonald Had a Farm." Have the chil-
        dren make the appropriate animal sounds. Use
        all the ones from the story (you can skip the

ant!) and add any others you have puppets for
(or make flannelboard animals).

References

Record Albums:

Rimsky-Korsakov, Nikolai. "The Flight of the Bumblebee."
Holiday for Strings. Arthur Fiedler and the Boston Pops. RCA
Victor LSC 2885.

Rubinstein, Anton. "Kamenoi Ostrow." *The Longine Sympho-
nette's Treasury of the World's Most Honored Music.* Columbia
XTV 82037.

Tchaikovsky, Peter. Serenade for Strings. *The Wonderful Waltzes
of Tchaikovsky.* Morton Gould and the Chicago Symphony
Orchestra. RCA Victor LSC 2890.

————. "Waltz and Apotheosis" from *The Nutcracker Suite. The
Wonderful Waltzes of Tchaikovsky.* Morton Gould and the Chicago Symphony Orchestra. RCA Victor LSC 2890.

————. "Waltz of the Flowers" from *The Nutcracker Suite. The
Wonderful Waltzes of Tchaikovsky.* Morton Gould and the Chicago Symphony Orchestra. RCA Victor LSC 2890.

————. "Waltz" from *Eugene Onegin. The Wonderful Waltzes of
Tchaikovsky.* Morton Gould and the Chicago Symphony Orchestra. RCA Victor LSC 2890.

Books (by Esphyr Slobodkina):

Billy the Condominium Cat. Addison-Wesley, 1967.

Caps for Sale. Scholastic, 1984.

Pezzo the Peddler and the Circus Elephant. Abelard-Schuman, 1967.

Pezzo the Peddler and the Seven Silly Thieves. Abelard-Schuman,
1969.

Pinky and the Petunias. Abelard-Schuman, 1959.

The Wonderful Feast. Lothrop, Lee and Shepard, 1954.

22.

Conclusion

When Spencer Shaw wrote about the difficulty of expressing in words the many techniques he employed and sought to perfect in the "selection, preparation and use of stories with recorded musical background," he may have hit upon the reason there is so little material available on the subject. His article ("Recorded Magic For Story Hours") in the October 1958 issue of *Top of the News* makes one feel that it would be much easier for people to sit down in a room together with piles of records and books and experiment with combinations of things.

Nevertheless, a book on the subject could, I believe, be useful in getting others to try for themselves some of the ideas discussed, and in encouraging them to experiment with music and stories on their own.

One way to get a feeling for how to do this would be to buy or borrow the Handel Harp Concerto mentioned in the opening chapter. Then read *Harry, the Dirty Dog* out loud to yourself without the music, then again with the music. Something magical happens. This is not to imply that straight storytelling isn't a wonderful event in itself, of course, but I do believe that the music adds another dimension. It helps create a mood. It stimulates and holds interest, and somehow quiets and focuses audiences' attention. It can enable librarians, teachers, or puppeteers to work with younger audiences by extending their attention spans. It helps cultivate a life-long skill and interest in reading, in stories, in books, in using libraries. And it certainly adds an element of cultural enrichment by exposing very young children to good music.

I have seen all of these results, so I know at firsthand that they are true. Some people have expressed concern to me that mixing in music might interfere with the storytelling. If it is not done right, I'm sure this could happen, but I feel certain, from

149

my experience, that it doesn't take a lot of trial and error to develop a flair for this type of programming. We're basically dealing with good stories, good music, and generally positive results. There is little to be afraid of here, other than the "newness" of it if you are a traditional storyteller.

As Spencer Shaw discovered, there is a whole world of benefit and enrichment for children that can result from enhancing stories with music. I hope you will use the ideas in this book as starting points for experimentation and successes of your own.

Frances Smardo of the Dallas Public Library and John Curry of North Texas State University published a scientific study in 1982 titled *What Research Tells Us About Storyhours and Receptive Language*. This study gives us some hard data about the value of story programs in relation to educational gains.

On the Test of Basic Education, the researchers found a significant difference in the receptive language skills (listening for understanding) of children who attended storyhours compared to children the same age who did not. The live story hours were found more effective than any other, significantly more effective than video story hours.

Smardo also mentioned that Head Start children had a real spontaneous ability with and proclivity toward rhythm and music, stating that this is an interesting area for further research.

She pointed out that three-, four-, and five-year-old children made the most dramatic gains in receptive language skills, concluding that public libraries should stress story hours for this particular age group. Her earlier point about children's natural tendencies toward music backs up my observation that music enables us to work with younger children than we might otherwise work with.

I noted at the start of this book that parents are encouraged to take out plenty of books after the programs to read to their children at home. Smardo found that reading to children makes them sensitive to the features of book language, and is probably more valuable to the beginning of school reading than is teaching phonics or sight vocabulary.

Children from book-oriented homes, she says, are more

likely to learn to read before school and to progress rapidly in reading skills when they do go to school. They develop a framework for the reading comprehension process.

If any of the ideas I have developed regarding the use of music with children's programming contribute to these far-reaching goals as discussed in the Dallas study, this book will have served a useful purpose.

The work that is being done by children's librarians and others working with children is profoundly important, as the study tries to prove with statistics. Anything we can do to add a little enchantment, a little more effectiveness, or simply more enjoyment is a worthwhile task.

23.

Quick Reference Section:

A list of pairings of stories and music discussed in this book

1. Harry the Dirty Dog
   - *Harry the Dirty Dog* (Zion)
     Concerto for Harp and Orchestra in B-flat Major, first movement (Handel)

2. Monkey Face
   - *Monkey Face* (Asch)
     Variations on a Theme by Rossini (Chopin)

3. Rabbits
   - "Br'er Rabbit and the Gizzard Eater"
     "Fiddle Faddle" (Leroy Anderson)
   - *The Adventures of Peter Rabbit* (Potter)
     Minuet (Boccherini)
   - *The Velveteen Rabbit* (Williams)
     Canon (Pachelbel)

4. Nightmares and Monsters
   - *There's a Nightmare In My Closet* (Mayer)
     Lullaby (Brahms)
   - *Too Many Monsters* (Meddaugh)
     "In the Hall of the Mountain King" (Grieg)
   - *Where the Wild Things Are* (Sendak)
     "Over the Waves" (Rojas)
   - *Weeny Witch* (DeLage)
     Ride of the Valkyries (Wagner)
     Barcarole (Offenbach)

5. Teddy Bears, Real Bears, and Monkeys
   - *Corduroy* (Freeman)
     Liebestraum no. 3 (Liszt)

152

- *A Kiss for Little Bear* (Minarik)
  Melody in F (Anton Rubinstein)
- *Curious George* (Rey)
  Eine Kleine Nachtmusik (Mozart)
- *Curious George Goes to the Aquarium* (Rey)
  Concerto in C for Flute and Harp (Mozart)

6. Slithery Snake Music
   - *Crictor* (Ungerer)
     Clarinet Concerto, first movement (Mozart)

7. Tall Tales
   - Pecos Bill stories
     Rodeo (Aaron Copland)
   - Paul Bunyan stories
     "San Antonio Rose"
   - John Henry stories
     "Shenandoah"
   - Windwagon Smith stories
     "Don't Fence Me In"
   - Davy Crockett stories
     "Bonanza" theme
   - Stormalong stories
     "The Sea and the Ship" (Rimsky-Korsakov)
     from *Scheherazade*

8. The Sea
   - *Swimmy* (Lionni)
     "The Aquarium" from *Carnival of the Animals* (Saint-Saens)
   - *Harry by the Sea* (Zion)
     Blue Danbue Waltz (Strauss)
   - *Bobby Shafto's Gone to Sea* (Taylor)
     "Blow the Man Down" (instrumental)
   - *Burt Dow, Deep Water Man* (McCloskey)
     "Skaters' Waltz" (Waldteufel)

9. Speed and Action
   - *Harriet and the Roller Coaster* (Carlson)
     "The Flight of the Bumble Bee" (Rimsky-Korsakov)

- *Nutty's Birthday* (Schumacher)
  "Can Can" (Offenbach)
- *The Gingerbread Man*
  Minute Waltz (Chopin)
- *Miss Tessie Tate* (Berg)
  William Tell Overture (Rossini)

10. Spooks, Witches, and Goblins
    - *Funnybones* (Ahlberg)
      "Fossils" from *Carnival of the Animals* (Saint-Saens)
    - *Tailypo, a Ghost Story* (Galdone)
      Les Preludes (Liszt)
    - *Spooky Night* (Carlson)
      "Danse Macabre" (Saint-Saens)
    - *Old Mother Witch* (Carrick)
      Symphony no. 8 (Unfinished) (Schubert)
    - *Suppose You Met a Witch* (Serralier)
      "Night on Bare Mountain" (Mussorgsky)
    - *Tilly Witch* (Freeman)
      "Sabre Dance" (Khachaturian)

11. Valentine's Day Programs
    - *The Valentines Bears* (Bunting)
      Piano Concerto no. 2, second movement (Rachmaninoff)
    - *Cinderella*
      "Recuerdos de la Alhambra" (Tarrega)
    - "The Owl and the Pussycat" (Lear)
      "Asturias" (Albeniz)
    - Poems from *It's Valentines Day* (Prelutsky, ed.)
      "Pizzicata Polka" (Strauss)

12. Other Special Days
    - *Hanukkah Money* (Aleichem)
      "Tzena, Tzena, Tzena"
    - *Little Bear's Thanksgiving*
      "September Song"

- *A Rabbit for Easter* (Carrick)
  Grand Sonata for Flute and Guitar (Giuliani)
- "Washington and the First Flight in America"
  Holiday Puppets (Ross)
  "El Capitan" (Sousa)
- "The Shoemaker and the Elves" (Grimm)
  Messiah Overture (Handel)

13. Royalty
    - "The Emperor's New Clothes" (Andersen)
      "Pomp and Circumstance March" no. 1 (Elgar)
    - "Puss in Boots"
      "The Waltzing Cat" (Leroy Anderson)
    - *King Midas and the Golden Touch* (Perkins)
      Concerto in E-flat Major for Trumpet (Haydn)
    - "The Princess and the Pea" (Andersen)
      Air on a G String (Bach)
    - *The King's Stilts* (Seuss)
      Trumpet Voluntary (Clark)

14. Off the Wall Stories and Music
    - *The Stupids Have a Ball* (Allard)
      "Holiday for Strings" (Spike Jones)
    - *The Stupids Die* (Allard)
      "Cocktails for Two" (Spike Jones)
    - *The Adventures of Albert the Running Bear* (Isenberg)
      Hungarian Rhapsody no. 2 (Liszt)
    - *Silly Goose* (Kent)
      "Perpetual Motion" (Ries)
    - *Five Minutes' Peace* (Murphy)
      "The Elephant" from *Carnival of the Animals* (Saint-Saens)
    - *Tell Us, Amelia Bedelia* (Parish)
      Symphony no. 94 *(Surprise),* second or third movement (Haydn)

15. Dance
    - *Isadora* (Silver)
      "In the Mood" (Glenn Miller)

- *My Ballet Class* (Isadora)
  "Waltz of the Swans" (Tchaikovsky)
- *The Dancing Class* (Oxenbury)
  Les Sylphides (Chopin)
- *The Story of Ferdinand* (Leaf)
  "Waltz of the Flowers" (Tchaikovsky)
- *The Dancing Man* (Bornstein)
  "Arabian Dance" from *Nutcracker Suite* (Tchaikovsky)
- *Dance Away* (Shannon)
  "Gold and Silver Waltz" (Lehar)
- *Harriet's Recital* (Carlson)
  "Dance of the Sugar Plum Fairies" from *Nutcracker Suite* (Tchaikovsky)

16. Caldecott Award Winners
    - *The Girl Who Loved Wild Horses* (Goble)
      New World Symphony, 3rd movement (Dvořák)
    - *Shadow* (Cendrars/Brown)
      "Into Yam" (Miriam Makeba)
    - *A Story, A Story* (Haley)
      "Dubula" (Miriam Makeba)
    - *The Egg Tree* (Milhous)
      Symphony no. 6 *(Pastoral)*, first movement (Beethoven)
    - *A Tree is Nice* (Udry)
      "Dance of the Blessed Spirits" (Gluck)
    - *Make Way for Ducklings* (McCloskey)
      "Colonel Bogey's March"
    - *Sylvester and the Magic Pebble* (Steig)
      "Spring Song" (Mendelssohn)
    - *Finders Keepers* (Lipkind)
      Violin Concerto, third movement (Mendelssohn)
    - *The Funny Little Woman* (Mosel)
      "Sukiyaka"

17. Fables and Folk Tales
    - "Rapunzel"
      "The Girl With the Flaxen Hair" (Debussy)

- "The Six Swans"
  "The Swan of Tuonela" (Sibelius)
- "Sleeping Beauty"
  "Reverie" (Debussy)
- "East of the Sun and West of the Moon"
  Piano Concerto, first movement (Grieg)

18. Orchestrating Dr. Seuss
    - "Too Many Daves"
      Bassoon Concerto, first movement (Vivaldi)
    - "What Was I Scared Of?"
      "Anitra's Dance" from *Peer Gynt Suite* (Grieg)
    - *Dr. Seuss' Sleep Book*
      "Prelude to the Afternoon of a Faun" (Debussy)
    - "I Can Lick 30 Tigers Today"
      "Tiger Rag"
    - *Horton Hears a Who*
      "Voices of Spring" (Strauss)
    - *Horton Hatches the Egg*
      Symphony no. 101, second movement (Haydn)
    - *Green Eggs and Ham*
      Horn Concerto no. 1 first movement (Mozart)

19. Orchestrating Bill Peet
    - *Ella*
      "The Jolly Coppersmith" (Calliope music)
    - *Randy's Dandy Lions*
      "The Jolly Cobbler" (Calliope music)
    - *Encore for Eleanor*
      "The Thunderer" (Sousa)
    - *Merle the High-flying Squirrel*
      "Funeral March of a Marionette" (Gounod)
    - *The Gnats of Knotty Pine*
      "The Flight of the Bumble Bee" (Rimsky-Korsakov)
    - *Cyrus the Unsinkable Sea Serpent*
      "La Mer" (Debussy)

- *Hubert's Hair-Raising Adventure*
  "Cacklin' Sax" (Boots Randolph)
- *The Whingdingdilly*
  "Charlie Brown" (Boots Randolph)

20. Moonlight Sonatas
    - *Moongame* (Asch)
      Moonlight Sonata, first movement (Beethoven)
    - *Mooncake* (Asch)
      "Clair de Lune" (Debussy)
    - *Song of the Swallows* (Politi)
      "La Golondrina" (The Swallow)
    - "The Moon in the Mill Pond" (Harris/Disney)
      "Moonlight Serenade" (Glenn Miller)
    - *Time of Wonder* (McCloskey)
      Symphony no. 6, storm and clearing sequence (Beethoven)
    - *Moon Tiger* (Root)
      Symphony no. 94 *(Surprise)*, second movement (Haydn)

21. Russians
    - *Caps for Sale* (Slobodkina)
      Serenade for Strings (Tchaikovsky)
    - *The Wonderful Feast* (Slobodkina)
      "Kamenoi Ostrow" (Rubinstein)